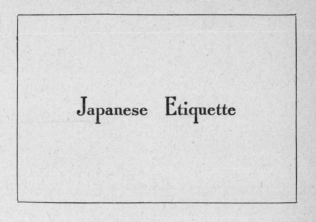

Japanese   Etiquette

A JAPANESE DRAWING ROOM

You are cordially invited to
a reading of

Japanese Etiquette
An Introduction

by

The World Fellowship Committee
of the Young Women's Christian Association
of Tokyo, Japan

Published by
The Charles E. Tuttle Company
of Rutland, Vermont and Tokyo, Japan

Representatives
Continental Europe: BOXERBOOKS, INC., Zurich
British Isles: PRENTICE-HALL INTERNATIONAL, INC., London
Australasia: PAUL FLESCH & CO., PTY. LTD., Melbourne
Canada: M. G. HURTIG LTD., Edmonton

Published by the Charles E. Tuttle Company, Inc.
of Rutland, Vermont and Tokyo, Japan with
editorial offices at Suido 1-chome, 2-6
Bunkyo-ku, Tokyo, Japan

Library of Congress
Catalog Card No. 59-9828

International Standard Book No. 0-8048-0290-4

First edition, 1955
Seventeenth printing, 1971

Printed in Japan

Contents

~ v ~

CONTENTS

CONTENTS

May We Introduce Ourselves

This book was conceived and an earlier version written a few years before the late war in order to meet the needs of American-born Japanese who at that time came in large numbers to study their parents' fatherland. It was also intended to be of help to the many foreign friends interested in our country. But just as it was ready to be sent to the printers, the war broke out and our dreams of what this book might bring about were all shattered.

Now peace reigns again. Our country has become a member of the family of nations. We have been touched by the interest and love towards our country shown by our foreign friends even through the difficult days after the war. Just recently when our committee held two series of lectures on Japanese living and culture, we were amazed at the interest shown by the guests. It is at the request of these friends that we have again resolved to present our material in book form to help those who are so earnest in their study of our country.

Our book has been written simply to introduce the etiquette of our everyday life to Westerners, both men and women. People throughout the world all follow different modes of living, and in doing so practice all kinds of etiquette as an integral part of their social life. However, we do not think that basic feelings differ so much between different peoples. We know that the basis of true courtesy is the same in every land and that we can understand each other if we are given the chance. But just because of the superficial differences we often fail to comprehend the good will of others, and, so many times, stand apart as strangers only through lack of understanding.

~ x ~

It is our sincere wish that this book may provide you with keys to our Japanese living—the everyday etiquette of Japan—and ultimately to the underlying spirit of our country, thereby helping to bring about a still greater understanding across all boundaries.

We have selected for this book, then, only those points in our everyday etiquette which are perhaps different from those in Western countries, though sometimes we have included Japanese expressions needed in general social situations. It is not a complete book of Japanese etiquette: it omits the very rigid and formal etiquette of the past and the Western ways quite generally and increasingly adopted by Japan even before the war. We have included the arts of flower arrangement and tea ceremony even though they may be considered outside the sphere of etiquette, because we feel that they are in many ways the quintessence of Japanese manners. We have also included a general outline of annual events in Japan.

First, though, there are two particularly delicate differences between Eastern and Western manners which we believe we should make clear at once in

this introduction, in order to prevent a passing un-
easiness or even some ill will between well-meaning
Westerners and welcoming Japanese. One, probably
the most difficult for the Western guest, occurs at
the very entrance to the place of hospitality and
concerns the removal of one's footgear before going into a Japanese home. This is no mere formality
but both a necessity and a courtesy for the sake of
cleanliness indoors and care of the softer Japanese
flooring, especially the typical *tatami* (floor mats).
Also, starting with the entrance of a guest, the
Japanese-type roles played by the host and hostess
differ from Western counterparts in certain strict
ways which we hope our friends will accept without
misgiving.

Specific questions as to what a foreigner would
or should do on certain occasions, we have tried to
meet with helpful answers. On the whole we
feel that it is quite unnecessary for a foreigner to
try to follow Japanese customs entirely. In many
cases, we should like you to follow your own customs, for many of our Japanese customs are already
changing and others are complicated and needlessly

expensive, a situation that we ourselves should alter. All in all it should not be difficult for us to meet on a common ground of give and take.

This book was originally compiled by a group of Japanese women and American-born Japanese girls : Midori Hasumoto, Suzue Ikebuchi, Reiko Ito, Kinue Kan, Haruko Miyagawa, Yuka Otsuki, Tamaki Nao, and Yoneko Tanaka. Though by no means special students of etiquette, we felt, while studying and doing this work together, confident that we had been able to discover points in Japanese life that people abroad wondered about and wished to know more of. Doing the work together was a great joy in itself. Many a gentle laugh was brought forth time after time in our conversation as we recognized both differences and similarities in the customs of the East and West.

Such is the origin of this book. Now, on the occasion of its birth, we wish to extend our deep appreciation and heartfelt thanks to those friends who have so kindly encouraged and assisted us by listening to our own many questions, and also by helping with our manuscript. Especially do we owe thanks to Mr. Yoshichika Tokugawa, the authority on Japanese etiquette; Mrs. Marguerite Iwamoto and Mr. Roland A. Mulhauser, who checked our English; and the Charles E. Tuttle Company, our appreciative and cooperative publisher. The illustrations are by Miss Etsu Sakurai, to whom we express our special thanks. For the sake of all our helpers we hope our book will serve its purpose.

We believe that, in spite of certain inevitable and desirable changes modernizing us, without the genuine Japanese spirit a certain grace and beauty would pass from our Japanese lives.

We are extremely glad of this opportunity to meet you through this book and, with suggestions from you for a new edition, we shall be still happier, knowing that this is but a first meeting leading to real understanding and friendship between us.

So, may we begin to introduce ourselves to you?

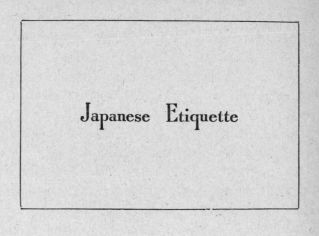

Japanese   Etiquette

Chapter One

Salutations

All salutations in Japan are expressed by bows. It is the way we greet our friends, pay respect to each other, express thanks, apologize, ask favors of each other, and say goodbye. There are three degrees of bowing; the *saikeirei*, now very seldom used; the ordinary salutation; and the light bow.

Types of Bows

THE *SAIKEIREI* — This word means " highest form

of salutation," the bow being made slowly, deeply, and very formally, expressing profound obeisance. Since our highest respect was paid to the Emperor, this *saikeirei* was used only toward him. With circumstances changed after the war, it has been abolished. Now Japanese make the same ordinary respectful bow toward the Emperor as toward others.

THE ORDINARY SALUTATION — In bowing while sitting on the floor Japanese fashion, which will be described below, one places the hands on the floor, palms down, four to six inches apart and bows between the hands, bringing the head to within four to six inches of the floor. Care should be taken to bow quietly.

In bowing while standing, we stand upright and look forward, then bend the body to about a thirty-degree angle while lowering the hands, palms down, to the knees, and, after a short pause, lift the

head quietly. Care
should be taken not to
bend at a sharp angle
at the hips or to lower
the head only. It is
most important that a
bow be made quietly
and courteously.

THE LIGHT BOW — It
has been the custom of the Japanese to bow a great
deal. Oftentimes in the past when on a visit and
greeting each other, those who met bowed after
every few words. But in the present day this is
considered too complicated, and after the first salutation is made it is thought better to use only the
light bow. In making a light bow, whether standing or sitting, the body should be bent at a fifteen-
degree angle. It is not enough to nod only. The
hands may be left at the sides or drawn closer to the
knees.

Examples of Salutations

ON THE STREET — In the past it was the proper etiquette in Japan, on meeting a senior who was on foot while one was riding in a vehicle, to alight from the vehicle and make a bow. Also it has been the custom when meeting on the street to take off coats and scarves before extending greetings. This may still be seen done on the streets of even such modern cities as Tokyo, but in the present age our new etiquette does not require it. The only point that must be remembered is that when meeting a senior on the street one must always be sure to stop first and then bow. If one arm is occupied, the other, even singly, should be drawn palm-down properly to the knees.

Bows made on the street are made a little higher than those made indoors. This is for obvious reasons; Japanese also laugh at funny extremes of formalities still practiced in public places, at times blocking traffic. There is something unintentionally comic when one party bows, then, lifting his head and finding the other still bowing, hurries to lower his head again; it is indeed a difficult art to watch each other and shade off the bowings with respect appropriate to the parties meeting!

IN A PASSAGEWAY — In the office and in school when meeting one's senior for the first time in the day one must make the ordinary bow, and even when meeting the same person many times a day one must still bow, though then only the lighter bow is necessary.

On meeting one's seniors in a narrow hallway one should pause at the left, bow slightly, and await the other's passage. If starting up a stairway, one should return to the bottom and there await the passage of the other person. At all other times one goes to the left and waits.

IN THE HOME — In Japan whenever one's parents are going out or returning, one goes to the door to send them off or to welcome them back. This is something that is always done, perhaps more so in Japan than in the West, for filial piety is still one of the leading virtues of family life and deep respect is always paids to one's parents in the home.

One is accustomed to say, *Itte mairimasu,* "I am going," when leaving the house, and, *Tadaima,* "I am just back," when returning. These are the salutations that we always use and must never forget to use in Japanese everyday life.

AT THE SHRINE — Salutations made at shrines and temples are called *hairei.* According to strict ceremonial rites, there are many difficult ways and forms, but the ordinary worshipper may proceed as follows : First cleanse the hands with the water provided, then go in front of the shrine and make a light bow, move forward a little, bow two times, clap twice, move one step backwards, and make a light bow. However, instead of the two bows and claps, which is an old Japanese custom, just one bow may be made.

Chapter Two

Visiting

Until the beginning of this century most Japanese women were accustomed to staying at home and very seldom went out to public gatherings or parties, which were primarily masculine affairs. However, they sometimes visited relatives or friends to talk and partake of tea and cakes. Also they made formal calls. At that time, when visiting was the only social activity of Japanese women, they were taught from their youth when and how they should call. For that reason the etiquette of paying calls may be especially interesting to anyone observing

Japanese customs. In any case, the formalities described below are basically the same for both men and women, the women being particularly punctilious in this observance.

Occasions for Calling

There are of course the typical kinds of calls: business calls and formal calls. Formal calls are especially appropriate for purposes of congratulations on a wedding, birth, or promotion, for expressing sympathy, and for season's greetings. Season's greetings are ordinarily made at the New Year, mid-year, and year-end. As is probably the case the world over, the New Year salutation expresses hopes for a happy life; mid-year and year-end salutations, however, are more peculiarly Japanese, and express one's respect during the hot and cold seasons. When kind-hearted people call to inquire after illness or accident, we must return such calls to express our thanks. Upon being invited to a tea ceremony in the traditional manner, one must call only at the inviter's *genkan* (house entrance) to express thanks and give the answer whether or not one can accept. Also, three to five days after the dinner or ceremony, the guest must call again to express thanks. Calling in person is the most polite way in which to pay one's respects and express appreciation.

Another necessary call is for salutation when one has moved into a new neighborhood. It is customary for either the husband or the wife, more often than not the wife, to do this in person at the entrance of the neighbors' houses on either side of the newcomer and the three houses opposite. In olden days we distributed buckwheat noodles, or coupons for such noodles, as a present, but nowadays we need not do so. Noodles seem to have been used to symbolize the hope for an acquaintance which would be long even if slight, just as the noodles are long and thin. With or without noodles, this call is made within three days after the move. On the other hand, if we are the recipient of such a call, we must not fail to return the greeting, likewise in person, at the new neighbor's entrance. In this case it is not necessary to return gifts even when we are given the noodles or other small things. If we are asked to enter the house during such a call, we may do so and sit and talk for a little while, unless the hostess seems too busy.

Time for Calling

Usually, following dictates of courtesy or common sense, we do not call during, immediately before or after a meal, or before working hours in the morning, nor at night. Unless the matter is pressing, we do not visit in extremely hot or cold weather, because of the discomforts connected with usual Japanese living. It is better not to call on national holidays, Sundays, and other holidays without an appointment, because others might be planning something of their own. Especially, it is best to avoid calling on the last day of the month, that day being by long custom one on which household bills are paid, an activity which keeps housewives very busy. Most Japanese women have no " at home " day. Friendly calls or business calls may be arranged by telephone. But formal calls, especially upon a senior person, should not be arranged by telephone.

With exceptions, especially after definite appointment, visiting, for women, falls between ten in the morning and four in the afternoon. The leisurely, freer times of the past have changed for Japanese too. In fact, men or business-women may necessarily have to call in the evening, on Saturday afternoon, or on Sunday. If the host or hostess is not at home, cards or gifts may be left at the entrance.

At the Entrance

Before the war, most Japanese homes of the upper class had two entrances, the main entrance (*omotegenkan*) for guests and the master of the house and a subsidiary entrance (*nai-genkan*) for intimate friends or relatives and family members. On formal visits we always call at the main entrance. The subsidiary entrance may be used more informally when calling on intimate friends or relatives.

After taking off scarf and gloves at the door, according to Japanese custom, we push the bell, if there is one, or call out : *Gomen kudasai.* " Excuse me." If there is no lock on the door, we open it quietly after having called out—for in a Japanese household there is sure to be a *rusuban* (someone who stays at home to watch the house).

We make a light bow to the maid as we present our card or give our name.

Upon Being Asked to Enter

When we are greeted with, *Dôzo o-agari kudasai,* " Please come in," we naturally answer, *Dewa shitsurei itashimasu,* " Thank you, I will." We remove our shoes, usually leaving them as they are, facing toward the interior of the house. It is for the maid, the hostess, or the host to arrange them so that the toes point outward toward the road to facilitate our getting into them on leaving. A woman guest, however, may often do this herself so as not to trouble the hostess. A guest must never turn his or her back to the host or hostess while removing shoes, and only the hand should be used in arranging them, never the foot.

Traditionally, polite guests removed coats before opening the door, but nowadays we do so inside the entrance just after we are asked to enter. For Westerners, when the room is not warm enough, it is permissible to enter the room wearing coats with the apology: *Shitsurei itashimasu.* " I beg your pardon."

If we are offered slippers, we put them on and follow the maid into the room.

It is not necessary for women to remove their hats, but it is better to do so if we are entering a Japanese-style house inasmuch as Japanese women do not ordinarily wear hats at any time.

Upon Entering the Room

When we have been invited in, we should not gaze curiously about while we are being conducted to the reception room. We simply look down three feet ahead as we walk. If the reception room is floored with Japanese-style *tatami* we take off our slippers before entering. In a foreign-style room this is not necessary.

A Japanese floor as you know is covered with *tatami*. The size of the *tatami* is six feet by three feet. It has a foundation of hard-pressed straw two inches thick and is covered with a mat woven with rush and bordered with linen strips which are black or brown or sometimes white with blue designs. The size of a Japanese room is always stated according to the number of its mats. For example we refer to an eight-mat room (*hachi-jô*) or ten-mat room (*jû-jô*).

The doors of a Japanese room are always either *shôji* (sliding paper doors) or *fusuma* (heavier sliding doors). *Shôji* are used on the side of the room near the *engawa,* which is sort of a porch-corridor, and *fusuma* are used between rooms to separate them into areas of privacy.

Upon entering the reception room we first close the *shôji* or *fusuma*, not forgetting that one always kneels when opening or closing a Japanese sliding door. After that, we bow first to the host or hostess and next to any guests who might be present. In case we are the only guest and the host or hostess follows us into the room, he or she closes the door.

In lowering oneself to the *tatami* for sitting, the toes of one foot are drawn back or brought forward slightly, the knees bent quietly and placed in turn on the floor. At this time the body should not lean forward. In the correct sitting posture the big toes are placed one on top of the other beneath the body. A man's knees are placed about three or four inches apart, a woman's close together; then with the body up straight, one looks toward the front. The man's hands are placed on the thigh, the woman's clasped lightly in front. When in foreign clothes it is permissible for men to sit with their legs crossed after asking permission and for women to relax the knees a little by pointing the feet out sideways But such easy postures must

never be used when in Japanese clothes or in front
of a person of high position.

After Entering the Room

A true Japanese drawing-room (*zashiki*) has an
alcove (*tokonoma*), a book-shelf (*shoin*), and zig-zag
shelves (*chigaidana*). The principal seat of honor
is in front of the *tokonoma*, followed by that in front
of the *shoin*, and then that in front of the *chigaidana*. The seat nearest the entrance is the lowest
position, and the guest should normally sit there
first until offered another seat. However, it would
be rude for anyone to occupy that seat if, by doing
so, he would get in the way of anybody coming into
or going out of the room. Under such circumstances,
we should sit elsewhere, but no one should ever
take the seat of honor in front of the *tokonoma*
until invited to do so by the host or hostess.

Women guests bow lightly when the maid brings
a cushion (*zabuton*) and in summer, a fan, but it is
better not to make use of them before the host or

hostess comes in. However, in cold weather, etiquette concedes the cushion, for the *tatami*, cooling in summer, is too cold for winter.

In the summer, when a twisted moist towel is presented, it is used for refreshing our hands, and may be used before the host or hostess comes in. It should not be used for the face or arms unless one is urged to do so by the host or hostess. After using the towel, we re-fold it neatly and return it to its container.

We bow lightly when the tea and cakes are served, but we do not partake of them before the host or hostess greets us.

Greeting Each Other

When the host or hostess enters the room, we slip quietly off the cushion onto the *tatami* floor, place our hands properly on the *tatami*, and wait until she takes her seat before voicing our salutations. The point to remember is that it is very impolite indeed to extend greetings while sitting on the cushion before having been properly welcomed.

After the salutations have been exchanged, the host or hostess will graciously remind us of the cushion. We then say a few words such as, *Gomen kudasaimase* or *Gomen kudasai,* "Pardon," the former being used by women and the latter by men, and take the cushion. To do so, we draw it a little towards us, rise on our knees a little, and slide gracefully onto it. However, if some senior person is present, we must never make use of a cushion before he or she does. Also it should be remembered that we must never use the cushion right away without saying those few words.

It is permissible to use the fan offered us or to warm our hands at the brazier (*hibachi*). We may also now take the tea and cakes. However, it is better to wait with both fan and food until after a few minutes of conversation and then say quietly a phrase of acceptance, *Itadakimasu,* "Thank you," with an accompanying bow, of course.

Should anyone, other than the servant, enter the room while we are conversing with the hostess, we always remove ourselves from the cushion onto the *tatami*. After the introductions we return to the cushion, but only after the senior person or persons present do so.

Tea and Cakes

Tea and cakes are a traditional part of Japanese hospitality, being served not only in homes but often in offices as well. When we are urged to drink the tea, we make a light bow, saying: *Itadakimasu.* "Thank you." We take up the teacup (*chawan*) with our right hand and place our left hand underneath, laying the fingers of the right hand lightly along the side. After  we have sipped the tea, quietly, we return the cup to the saucer (*chataku*) with our right hand. It is not in the best taste to sip tea or eat any other food noisily, although the practice is much more common in Japan than in America.

For the cakes the etiquette is different. We take the dish with our right hand and place it in the palm of our left hand. If no individual plates are provided, we use our " bosom paper " (*futokoro-gami*), which is a soft paper carried in the bosom of the kimono by both men and women. Hard sweets may be broken with the fingers and eaten with the right hand. If the sweet is soft, we cut it one bite at a time with the small fork or whatever is provided for the purpose before eating it. If there is another guest sitting next to us, with a light bow we should say, *Osaki ni,* " Before you," before we take the cake on our own plate or " bosom paper." We always say this *osaki ni* when we do anything before the person with us. When we prefer not to eat, it is permissible to say frankly : *Mô kekkô de gozaimasu.* " I have had plenty." If the hostess wraps the refreshment in paper and gives it to us, we are expected to take it home.

Typically the Japanese guest never eats before the host or hostess does. Hence the hostess should serve the guests and then serve herself and eat first. This delicately signifies that the guest regards the host or hostess as a senior. It is also said that the host or hostess by eating first symbolizes a traditional " testing for poison," thus assuring the guest that the refreshments are eatable.

In the past, Japanese families always offered dinner whenever a guest came, but nowadays, especially since the war, this custom has been dying out and only tea and sweets are offered. On business calls usually only tea is served. Many Westerners wonder whether they should serve tea to Japanese guests. To this again we should like to recommend that they follow their own customs and feelings, because we ourselves feel that this old custom of serving tea and cakes every time guests arrive is so complicated, under present-day circumstances, that a change should be made.

Preparing to Leave

If it is a first visit, we must take care not to

prolong our stay. We should plan to leave after thirty minutes at the most.

At a good break in the conversation it is proper to say : *Taihen nagaku o-jama wo itashimashita. Kore de shitsurei sasete itadakimasu.* " I have disturbed you for a very long time. Now I beg to be excused."

When we say goodbye we shift from the cushion to the *tatami* and, inclining the body, politely place our hands down in front of us. If our host or hostess tries to restrain us, we say with a bow : *Arigatô gozaimasu ga shitsurei sasete itadakimasu.* " Thank you, but please let me be excused."

To stand up, the hips should be raised first, with the back erect, then one foot drawn forward slightly, the body raised, and both feet drawn together, all of this being done quietly. One should not attempt to stand up directly in front of one's senior without first changing one's position.

If there are any elderly persons in the home we are visiting, we make sure to pay our respects to them prior to our departure.

Leaving

When we have finished paying our parting respects, we make another slight bow before leaving the room, then proceed to the *genkan* (entrance). We always make it a point to decline the offer to see us out. Particularly if there is another guest, it is necessary to be firmer in our declining, saying: *Dôzo o-kamai naku.* "Please do not worry about me."

At the entrance hall we bow again as we say thank you before taking our coat and our gloves, and excuse ourselves with the phrase : *Shitsurei itashimasu.* "Pardon me."

Some Japanese will not, even upon insistence, put on their coats and scarves until they have gone out of the gate, especially when they visit a senior. But it is permissible to put on a shawl or *katakake* (stole) if we are urged to do so.

When taking off house slippers, we make sure to leave them neatly arranged, toes facing away from the entrance for the convenience of the next visitor.

After we have put on our things, we bow again, this time very politely, and leave. In spite of remonstrances, a Japanese host or hostess always comes to see a guest off at the entrance, sometimes to the gate. When accompanied to the gate where a car may wait, it is polite to bow before we get in.

How to Present a Gift

The old Japanese custom of taking a gift whenever one called is slowly dying out, but there are still people who do this. It is a custom that should be altered, for sometimes the thought that a gift must be taken has made it irksome for the call to be made. Of course such gifts as fruit grown in one's garden or chestnuts sent from one's country home are lovely.

In the event that we have brought a gift with us, it should always be presented at the beginning of the call. We may hand it to the maid when we present our calling-card or give our name, or we may present it to the host or hostess after we have entered the reception room and finished our greetings.

According to the Japanese custom, the receiver does not open the gift in the presence of the giver. Now, however, we are more and more following the Western custom and, according to the occasion, often do open it, especially on such occasions as birthdays when the giver has selected the gift carefully.

In the Japanese Room

In a Japanese room care must be taken never to step on anything or to step over anything. Even the groove and the edging of the *tatami* should not be stepped on.

When speaking or handing something to a person who is sitting, one should sit down to do so; it is considered very rude to do otherwise.

When it is necessary to pass in front of a person

who is sitting, we do so on our knees, placing our hands in front of us and drawing both knees forward at the same time.

When we look at a bowl or any object while in a sitting position, upon picking it up, we hold it in both hands, with our arms braced against our knees, which are on the floor. In this way we can be sure not to let the object fall and break.

When rice or tea is served on a tray, we take them from the tray. But if other things are offered on a tray, we take the tray with both hands and put it down on the *tatami*, take the thing off, then return the tray.

When we are interested in ornaments on the *tokonoma*, such as the hanging picture, flower arrangement, or other decorative pieces, it is permissible to look at them after asking: *Haiken sasete itadaite yô gozaimasu ka?* "May I look at it?" We then look while sitting in front of the *tokonoma*, placing the hands forward on the *tatami*. But it is also permissible for men and Westerners to look while standing.

Thanks

After we have been guests at a luncheon, dinner, or afternoon tea, it is necessary to thank our hostess either by phone or letter as soon as possible. Or, again, if it is possible, we go to our hostess' home one or two days after the event and extend our thanks at the *genkan*.

As a matter of fact, for any particular kindness Japanese are quite punctilious about expressing thanks, in at least letter form. Women are particularly careful about such matters.

Chapter Three

Receiving Guests

Preparing the Room

When decorating a Japanese-style reception room, we hang a scroll (*kakejiku*) on the wall of the alcove (*tokonoma*) and place flowers or other decorative pieces in front of it. On the zig-zag shelves (*chigaidana*) we place a calligraphy-box (*suzuri-bako*), flowers, and other decorative pieces. But if there is a book-shelf (*shoin*), we place on it the calligraphy-box, along with books. We take good care that everything is neatly arranged and that everything is of course free from dust. We use linen cushions in summer and silk in winter.

At the Entrance

When an unfamiliar guest comes, we bow to him at the *genkan* and say quietly : *Irrasshaimase. Donata sama de irrasshaimasu ka?* "Welcome. May I ask who you are?" It is permissible at such times to ask for the visitor's calling-card by extending the card plate.

If this is not the first visit, we invite the guest in cordially with : *Yoku irrasshaimashita. Dôzo.* "Oh, how nice of you to call! Please come in." We help the guest to take off his coat, then hang it up or place it in the receptacle provided for foldable Japanese clothing.

After we have conducted the guest inside, we return to the *genkan* to make sure the guest's footwear (shoes, *zôri,* or *geta*) is arranged so that the guest may slip into it conveniently on the way out. If the guest came through the subsidiary entrance (*uchi-genkan*), the footwear must by all means be taken to the main entrance (*omote-genkan*) as a matter of courtesy to the guest.

Conducting the Guest Inside

Saying, *Dôzo kochira e o-tôri kudasaimase; torimida-shit*ᵃ *orimasu ga,* " Kindly come this way, and please excuse our disorder," we precede our guest into the house. This phrase is most appropriate for a hostess, it being more likely for a host simply to use only the first three words of the phrase. *Kudasaimase,* used here and in the next two quotations, is a feminine form, the masculine counterpart being simply *kudasai.*

We kneel before opening the sliding door (*fusu-ma*) or paper door (*shôji*), then with head slightly inclined say: *Dôzo o-tôri kudasaimase.* " Please enter." It is very important that the guest precede us into the room.

Placing a cushion at the position of honor in front of the *tokonoma,* we urge the guest to take it, saying: *Dôzo-ohiki kudasaimase.* "Please use this."

After our guest is seated, in summer we offer a fan (*uchiwa*) or in winter a brazier (*hibachi*). Then we may excuse ourselves with, *Chotto shitsurei itashimasu,* "Pardon me for a few moments," and retire to see to the refreshments.

Conversation and Refreshments

When the tea and cakes are ready, we return to the guest room and say: *Dômo shitsurei itashimashita.* "Pardon my rudeness in leaving you." With a slight bow, we too sit down—but not on a cushion if our guest happens to be a person of high status.

Again, for such a guest, it is necessary to renew our greeting very politely and cordially: *Yôkoso irrasshaimashita. Dôzo goyukkuri asobashite kudasaimase.* "I am so glad you have come. Please stay as long as you possibly can." Incidentally, a man in giving this greeting would omit the last two words, which have a feminine connotation.

We then bow to each other—and at last begin

real conversation. In Japan conversation is apt to begin only after the formalities have been carried out, an aspect of Japanese etiquette often disconcerting to the uninitiated Westerner.

We serve the tea and cakes first to the guest, with the politely derogatory words: *Socha de gozaimasu ga, dôzo*. "This is very poor tea, but please have some." Or we can simply say: *Ocha o dôzo*. "Please have some tea."

Anyone leaving the room uses the words: *Chotto shitsurei itashimasu*. "Pardon me a moment." And upon returning, he says, with an unobtrusive bow: *Shitsurei itashimashita*. "Forgive my rudeness."

Leaving

When the guest expresses the intention of leaving, it is customary to detain him with: *Ikaga de gozaimasu ka? Mô sukoshi goyukkuri nasaimasen ka?* "Oh, don't go yet. Won't you stay a little longer?" If the guest seems unable to stay longer, then one says: *Dewa nani mo o-kamai itashimasen deshita ga, kore ni okori naku mata dôzo.* "I have been a very poor hostess, but do come again."

If we have received a gift, we must remember especially to thank our guest very politely when he or she is leaving: *Kekkô na mono wo itadakima-shite makoto ni arigatô zonjimashita.* "Thank you for your very lovely gift."

When the guest rises to leave, it is the duty of the hostess to open the door, let the guest precede her out of the room, and accompany the guest to the house entrance. If the guest has left his or her slippers outside the room door, we should re-arrange them so that the guest may slip back into them again as easily as possible.

Chapter Four

Gifts

In Japan there are many lovely traditional and formal ways to give gifts, but according to present everyday etiquette it is not considered necessary for all of these customs to be followed strictly. For instance, though it has been customary in Japan to take a gift whenever making a call, this is one custom which should be altered. In any case it is considered impolite to give more than the occasion calls for, since the receiver will usually want to return a gift of equal value in the near future. When gifts are given nowadays it is often considered more appropriate to select not just formal ones but gifts that will more personally suit or please the receiver. Here, however, we will give a glimpse at some of the traditional Japanese gifts for special occasions, for there is something truly lovely in this traditional courtesy which the modern age would miss should it be eliminated entirely.

Gifts, being tokens of good will, should at all times be selected with care and thought. Gifts out of proportion to one's position, bought for sheer display, spoil the very spirit of giving.

Types of Gifts

In Japan, gifts are given at special seasons, on special occasions of felicitation or misfortune, when inquiring after illnesses and accidents, as an expression of appreciation of many kinds, or in token of farewell.

SEASONAL GIFTS — Traditionally gifts called *otoshidama* are exchanged at New Year's, *chûgen* at the mid-year, and *seibo* at the year-end. At present, however, these are often considered a needless expense and their complete abolition has been advocated. However, as a token of gratitude to those to whom we are indebted, it is obviously courteous to make seasonal calls and take presents.

The *otoshidama* is a gift signifying joy, taken when one calls at New Year's time. Mid-year gifts mark the season between the early and the middle part of July, and year-end gifts between the early and the middle part of December. Such gifts should be appropriate to the seasons: fans, Gifu lanterns, and other summery things for the hot season; for the cold season, food such as salmon, wild duck, pheasant, and *nara-zuke* (a Japanese pickle). All such traditional gifts are typical, although by no means is the choice so limited. Anything likely to be esteemed by the receiver and selected with care should be suitable.

At the mid-year and year-end, servants at places where one calls frequently are sometimes kindly remembered. The gift should always be presented through the employer or the mistress of the house.

FELICITOUS GIFTS — Presents are often made to

commemorate weddings, births, *hatsuzekku* (the first Doll Festival for a girl or the first Boys' Festival for a boy), promotions, openings for business, new constructions, recoveries from illness, and congratulatory occasions of any kind.

At any time, fresh fish or *katsuo-bushi* (dried bonito) may be used as tokens of good wishes. According to Shintoism the most precious offering is fresh fish, and it is from this custom that fresh fish is used on happy occasions. *Katsuo-bushi* is used for the same reason but also because the word *katsuo*, written in other characters, has the meaning " a man who wins." Japanese often use puns and have a sort of belief in their bringing good luck.

For congratulatory occasions red and white floss-silk is used sometimes. Whatever the choice, it should be with the receiver in mind, more or less in spite of the traditional formalities.

In return for such gifts, the receiver often still distributes traditional *seki-han* (rice cooked with red beans), *tsuru-no-ko-mochi* (red and white *mochi*), *katsuo-bushi*, red and white silken goods, kimono goods, or *fukusa* (small silk wrappers smaller than *furoshiki*). All these we Japanese call *uchi-iwai* which roughly signifies happiness in the home.

CONDOLENCE GIFTS — Gifts are offered to the spirits of the departed upon deaths and at times of Shinto and Buddhist masses for them. At the time of the death, money, enclosed in an envelope, is presented for the purchase of incense, flowers, and *tamagushi* (the *sakaki* branch used at a shrine). Incense sticks, fresh and artificial flowers, fruit, and sweets are also given.

In return, the receiver may distribute such Japanese things as *fukusa*, kimono-lining goods, tea, or *manjū* (bean-jam buns). Tea, which was first discovered by a Chinese priest and drunk as a medicine, has been used a great deal in connection with Buddhism, and since the tea flower is white and sorrowful, tea is given only on sad occasions. *Manjū* is used because it is a very plain undecorated cake. At the present day, however, the family of the deceased often omits the return of gifts entirely and instead presents a sum of money to some charity or public organization in which the deceased

was particularly interested, announcing such donation
in the letters of thanks which are sent out.

Wrapping the Gifts

All gifts are wrapped in white paper and tied
with *mizuhiki*, which is a special paper cord for
this purpose. There are many kinds of Japanese
paper that may be used for wrapping, such as
Danshi, *Hôsho*, *Torinoko*, *Sugiwaragami*, *Nishinouchi*,
Noriire, *Minogami*, and *Hanshi*. Ordinarily the *Hôsho*,
Noriire, *Hanshi*, or *Noshigami* are considered best.
This last-mentioned paper is used for very informal
cases only, and never towards one's seniors, since
the *mizuhiki* and a picture of a *noshi* are only
printed on it. It may be of interest to a Westerner
that "Japanese paper" is made entirely by hand
and never by machine. It is a very beautiful and
strong paper.

For formal occasions *Hôsho* or *Noriire* paper is
used, customarily two sheets of it, although for
wrapping a small gift a sheet folded in half may

~ 42 ~

be used. In the case of a very large present, the gift may be placed on a tray or a stand, on the two prescribed sheets of paper. For ordinary occasions just one sheet is necessary, and always for unhappy occasions just the one sheet is to be used.

Wrinkling must be avoided and the folding should be precise. Ordinarily the paper is wrapped so that the last fold comes on top of the package at the right-hand edge with the end of the paper extending all the way to the left-hand edge of the package. For unhappy occasions, however, the wrapping is reversed, with the last  fold on the top of the package at the left-hand edge and the end of the paper extending all the way to the right-hand edge of the package. One must be very careful about how this paper is folded, for people are very sensitive about it, and it would be rude indeed to send a gift folded as for an unhappy occasion on an ordinary or happy occasion. No paper is necessary in presenting fish or fowl;

the food should be arranged on leaves of Mongolia oak, Japanese cypress, Japanese cedar, pine, or nandina, and placed in a tray or basket.

THE MIZUHIKI — The *mizuhiki* long ago used to be just a band of paper, but as this was found inconvenient for keeping the gifts tied, a cord was made by rolling the paper together and wetting it with water (*mizu*). We now use the *mizuhiki* with several strands of these cords put together. This is the derivation of *mizuhiki*. Red, white, silver, and gold are the colors used.

For felicitous and ordinary occasions red-and-white or gold-and-red cords are used. Gold-and-silver cords are used only for weddings. Gifts with a red-and-white cord should be tied so that the red cord is on the right; and when using the gold-and-silver cord, the gold should be on the right. For obsequies white cords or black-and-white *mizuhiki* are used, with the black cord always on the right.

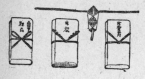

The *memusubi*, or butterfly knot, is used for almost all occasions. But for engagements, weddings, or obsequies the *mizuhiki* is always tied into a square knot, this implying in its permanence that such an occasion may never be repeated. Sometimes for weddings the so-called ear-shell knot is also used.

NOSHI — On gifts a *noshi* is always placed. Long ago it was the custom when giving gifts always to add some fresh fish or bird or seaweed, which was called *namagusa*, meaning raw food. But gradually this custom has become simplified and now in place of the fresh fish the *noshi* is used symbolically.

The *noshi* is made of ear-shell, a kind of abalone, stretched and dried. Since the ear-shell was used for food in the olden days, the *noshi* is not used with raw-food presents such as fish, shell fish, eggs, seaweed, and fowl. Nor is it used on obsequious occasions, in deference to Buddhist custom. For all other occasions, it is always placed on the top of the parcel at the right.

SUPERSCRIPTION — Parcels of all kinds should always be superscribed. There are many ways to do this, according to the occasion. *Kotobuki* (happiness) is appropriately used for happy occasions and *go-reizen* (to the spirit of the departed) for the unhappy; *jô* (superior) for one's seniors, *so-shina* (slight present) or *matsu-no-ha* (pine-leaf) for ordinary purposes, and sometimes *imo* (a trifle) for one's subordinates. Also, according to the purpose of the present, such words as *orei* (thanks), *omimai* (inquiry after illness), or *osembetsu* (farewell gift) are used. The sender's name is written at the center bottom. The recipient's name, if written, appears at the upper left, but may be omitted. When there are money enclosures the amount is usually specified on the back at the center bottom or on the back of the inner wrapping.

How to Offer and How to Receive

The gift is always taken out of the *furoshiki* (the silken wrapper) and presented with a statement appropriate to the occasion. It is bad etiquette to place it in a corner of the room, at the side of one's seat, or in the angle of a screen, as if forgotten.

In receiving a present, a statement of thanks of

course is made with a bow, and the gift is then drawn toward one and acknowledged with another bow.

For very formal occasions the gift is placed on a tray or a stand and is received along with the tray or stand. Whether a stand or *furoshiki* is used, this holder is always returned with two sheets of white paper, folded in quarters, called *o-utsurigami*, placed on the holder or enclosed in a wrapper. The paper is omitted, however, for weddings and for unhappy occasions.

The Japanese are very strict in their ways of acknowledging any favors they have received. *Orei* (presents of thanks) are taken as token thanks to a senior or a friend who has helped to find a position or a suitable teacher, to one who has acted as go-between, or to anyone who has helped in entertaining or has given some service. Even if the service is voluntary, whether amateur or professional, we always call on the person to express our thanks and take a gift. If the circumstance is such that we do not take a gift, we should at least call or write a letter of personal thanks.

Chapter Five

At the Table

The everyday Japanese meal usually consists of rice as the basic dish, soup, a few dishes of fish, meat, or vegetables, and some pickles, all eaten with chopsticks. Formerly the Japanese meal was always served on individual trays, but now with the changes in our homes, it is served at tables, often without the trays. In eating a Japanese meal there are some definite rules that must be followed. This need not alarm the Westerner, however, for these rules are not difficult, and if they are practiced faithfully, one will soon be able to eat a Japanese dinner with ease and grace, confident that he is not violating any basic rules of etiquette.

Ordinary Meals

Before starting to eat, one must always remember to say a few words, such as, *Itadakimasu*, " I shall begin eating," and make a light bow.

Because rice in Japan is considered the principal food, first of all, remove the cover of your individual rice bowl, which is still empty. Since this bowl is always placed at the left-hand side, take off the cover with your left hand and place it at your left facing upwards. Then with your right hand take off the cover of the soup bowl which is at your right and place it to the right. Whether or not you are the one to serve the rice, you must remember to do these two things in this order at the very beginning of a meal.

When the rice is to be served to you, take up the empty bowl at your place and, preferably with both hands, set the bowl on the tray extended to you. It is permissible to use only one hand if, for instance, your *kimono* sleeve is in the way, in which case you hold your right sleeve with your left hand and present your bowl with the right.

Next, after you have received from the server the rice bowl now filled with rice, you must always remember to place the bowl back upon the table or on your individual tray, for it is very bad form to begin eating the rice without doing this. Only after the rice bowl is placed back on the tray or table are the chopsticks taken up in the right hand and arranged with the left ready to be used. Then the rice bowl is taken up with the left hand and one or two mouthfuls of rice eaten. It is an old Japanese custom to begin with the rice, the principal food; but this does not mean that it always must be eaten first, for sometimes the soup may be taken first. (May we just add here that the preparation of a Japanese soup is an art in itself, and a cook is often judged by her ability to make soup. Hence a hostess is always pleased by having her soup praised.)

There are many accepted ways to hold a rice

bowl, but the best way is to put it on the four fingers of the left hand and let the thumb rest lightly on the brim of the bowl but not hooked into the food. Japanese themselves must learn from the beginning how to hold the chopsticks correctly, for unless one can hold them correctly, one will not be able to eat with ease or grace.

Now, after taking up the chopsticks and rice bowl and eating only one or two mouthfuls of rice, put down your bowl, and with the right hand take up the soup bowl and put it on the palm of the left hand. Some of the soup is drunk first, then some

of the contents eaten. Next, rice is eaten again, and then more soup or some other dish on the right-hand side. After this, anything may be eaten, except the pickles. The pickles are to be eaten at the end of the meal. This is because the taste of pickles is strong and if eaten first takes away the good taste of other foods. However, each dish must be alternated with the rice.

For the second helping, a bit of rice is left in the bowl. This shows that you have not yet finished your dinner, and the server will know that you wish another helping. If you wish only a light helping, say: *Okaruku negaimasu.* " Lightly please."

After you have received your second helping of rice or soup, don't forget to place the bowl back upon the tray or table before continuing your eating.

When one is finished with the rice, the last few grains are eaten, so that not one single grain of rice is left in the bowl. Upon seeing this, the server will know that you have finished, if this is a home in which this time-honored custom is still observed, and will serve tea in your rice bowl. Now it is time for the pickles. After the pickles are eaten, dip the tips of your chopsticks slightly in the tea to cleanse them, place them on the tray, and then drink your tea. When drinking now, it is graceful if you lift the bowl with your left hand and hold it with the right resting against its side, just as you would do when drinking tea from an ordinary Japanese cup.

After you have finished with the tea, the covers to the rice, soup, and any other bowls are replaced in order. During a meal the chopsticks, when not in use, should always rest at the right side of the tray protruding beyond the edge of the tray about one inch ; but now that the dinner is over, they should be laid in the tray to indicate that you are through. Now offer thanks for the dinner with, *Arigatô gozaimashita*, " Thank you very much," or, *Gochisô-sama de gozaimashita*, " You have given me quite a treat," and a bow.

Table Don'ts

Here are some Japanese table-etiquette don'ts :
1. *Don't* pick up chopsticks until one's seniors have taken theirs.
2. *Don't* scrape rice grains from the chopsticks.

3. *Don't* linger over the dishes undecided as to what to take next.

4. *Don't* take food from the soup without lifting the bowl from the tray.

5. *Don't* take food from dishes on the farther side without lifting up the dishes.

6. *Don't* take up dishes on the right side with the left hand or those on the left with the right.

7. *Don't* place food with liquid sauces on the rice or eat with the sauce dripping.

8. *Don't* pick up and bite off chunks of food that cannot be eaten in one mouthful, but cut them into smaller pieces with the chopsticks.

9. *Don't*, when pickles have been eaten with the *ochazuke* (tea poured over the rice), resume eating any remaining meat or fish.

10. *Don't* hold the rice bowl to one's mouth and shove in rice with the chopsticks except when eating *ochazuke* or rice with hot water poured over it.

11. *Don't* use your own chopsticks when helping

yourself from a serving dish. If there are no separate chopsticks (this will not be the case, however, at a formal dinner), either ask for some or reverse your own and use the opposite ends.

12. *DON'T* leave any rice uneaten in one's bowl. If unable to finish a full second serving, one should ask for only a light serving, saying, *Okaruku negaimasu.* "Lightly, please."

13. *DON'T* fail to lay down your chopsticks and stop eating while being given a second serving:

14. *DON'T* smack the lips, speak with the mouth full, or publicly use a toothpick.

Formal Dinners

Once you have mastered the foregoing rules for ordinary meals, the more detailed rules to be followed at formal dinners on ceremonial occasions will seem natural.

At a Japanese dinner party, as in any other country, the first consideration is to arrange the seating prop-

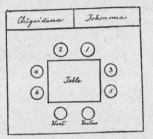

erly in accordance with the seniority and social position of the guests. In Japan the principal seat of honor is that now-familiar one in front of the *tokonoma*, and, unlike the European system, the host and hostess sit together at the lower end of the table.

The *honzenryôri* (a full course dinner), which is served on very formal occasions, consists of two soups and either five, seven, or ten entrees, and is served on four or occasionally even five trays : *suimonozen* (soup course), *honzen* (main course), *ninozen* (second course), *sannozen* (third course), and *shinozen* (fourth course). The *honzenryôri* is served very seldom nowadays ; ordinarily served is a more informal dinner with a menu not quite so set as that of the *honzenryôri*.

The following is a sample menu of such an informal dinner, consisting of seven items (five entrees plus rice and soup) :

An *omuko* consisting of *maguro sashimi*, *mejiso*,

oroshi-daikon, and *wasabi* (sliced raw tunny with perilla, grated radish, and grated horseradish).

A *yakimono* or *hachizakana* consisting of *ebodai sugatayaki* and *aotôgarashi aburayaki* (whole broiled seabream with fried green peppers).

A *nimono* consisting of *fukiyose-matsutake, ginnan, kuri,* and *ebi* (mushrooms, ginko nuts, chestnuts, boiled shrimp, and sesame with sugar or sweet wine and soy sauce).

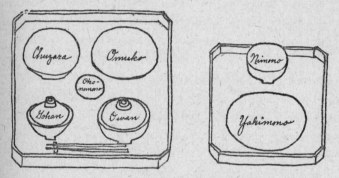

SEVEN-ITEM DINNER

An *owan* consisting of *tsukunedori, mitsuba,* and *matsuba yuzu* (clear soup with chicken balls, trefoil, and citron peel shaped as pine leaves).

A *chûzara* consisting of *shiba-ebi kimpura, ingen,* and *shôga* (shrimp 'kimpura' style with string beans and grated ginger).

A simple home dinner might typically consist of five items (three entrees plus rice and soup).

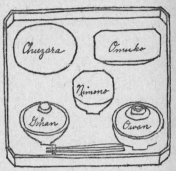

FIVE-ITEM DINNER

In the *honzenryôri* there is a definite order for the serving of the dinner, but in the informal dinner usually all the dishes are served at the same time. However, when *saké* (Japanese wine) is served, it precedes the dinner proper and is served with two or three dishes of relishes called *otôshi*; then comes the dinner; and finally, after the table has been cleared, the dessert.

With regard to the serving of *saké* a few pointers here might heighten the Westerner's enjoyment and avoid any embarrassment he might have over the formalities observed. First of all, on being served *saké*, one holds up his cup (*sakazuki*) to receive the *saké* and then takes a sip or at least puts it to his lips before putting it down. The second point to remember is never to serve oneself unless one has first picked up the *tokuri* (wine container) and served the others present. More likely than not someone will relieve you of the *tokuri* so that you will not have to serve yourself. It will very often happen that a guest, considered to be a senior person, will be offered the *saké* cup of the host or someone else present, in which case one is expected to accept the cup, to hold it while it is being filled, and to drink the *saké* from this cup. The cup need not be returned immediately but it should not be kept after the *saké* has been drunk. The cup is then returned to the person who presented it, and you, in turn, are expected to pick up the *tokuri* and serve him. Later you may wish to present your cup to the host or some honored guest or someone to whom you wish to pay respect, and it is perfectly all right to do this. When one does not wish to have any more *saké*, this is indicated by placing the *saké* cup on the table upside down.

If one does not wish to drink any *saké* it is not

necessary to do so. In fact, Japanese women usually do not drink *saké*. In such a case one simply puts the filled cup to one's lips and then pours the *saké* into a wash bowl called a *haisen*, if one has been provided. This same bowl, containing water, is used by the guests to rinse out their own *sakazuki* before offering it to anyone else.

In serving the informal dinner, the rice bowl still goes on the left and the soup on the right; in addition, all the shallow dishes go on the right and all the deeper ones on the left, except that of the *omuko*, which is placed at the right. The chopsticks are placed at the front of the tray (nearest the guest), with the tips (the ends used in eating) on a chopstick rest, if there is one. Since chopsticks are held in the right hand, their rest should naturally go on the left. In place of the Western-style finger bowl the *oshibori* is used at Japanese dinners. This is a small hand-towel, rinsed in either hot or cold water and wrung almost dry. It is not untwisted after wringing but is placed just as it is in a small basket and put beside each tray. While there is nothing in Japanese etiquette which corresponds to the Western-style napkin, there is a tendency to adopt the napkin along with many other forms of Western etiquette. More Japanese, though, use "bosom-paper" (*futokoro-gami* or *kaishi*). When visiting or going to dinners or tea ceremonies, one should always carry a supply of this "bosom-paper," so called because it is kept in a little case in one's bosom above the sash. It is most frequently made of *sugiwara* or rice paper and has many uses. For instance, as noted before, should you be served some cake on a very beautiful lacquer dish and are afraid you might scratch the dish, then you take the cake on the *kaishi* to eat it. Or when the tips of your chopsticks might soil your tray, you protect the tray by putting your chopsticks on the *kaishi*.

A point to be remembered as a guest at a dinner party is that the guest should sit as the host bids, and when everyone is seated and the host's greetings are over, the main guest begins the dinner, for only after the main guest has done so may the others take up their chopsticks.

Serving the Meal

When serving rice, one must always remember to serve it in more than one scoop, for to fill a bowl with a single scoop is considered too abrupt. One must also take care not to hold the bowl with the thumb inside it, just as in the West one should not put one's fingers in a cup or glass.

The thumb should not be hooked over the edge of the tray when serving. The server should hold the tray high enough so as not to breathe on the food or overlook the dishes. In the process of serving, the tray is placed before the knees of the server, from which position the food is taken and served to the guests. At this time the server is particularly careful to refrain from touching hair and clothing.

Chapter Six

Japanese Dress

Kimono in Relation to the Season

It has been the custom of the Japanese from olden times to adapt their dress to the different seasons rather than to the weather. The changes of clothes now occur, generally speaking, as follows : lined or double garments are worn from the first part of October to the latter part of May, and unlined or summer garments are worn from the first part of June to the latter part of September. During the coldest months, from November to

March, old people and children wear padded garments. Then again, during the short period in spring and autum when the lined garment is changed to the unlined, and vice versa — from the first to the latter part of May and from the first to the middle part of October — the *kimono* of flannel or light serge is worn, though only around the house or on a visit to an intimate friend, and never on formal occasions. Formerly no little ceremony accompanied these seasonal changes of clothing.

Bridal Attire

The usual dress of the bride is a black *furisode,* a long-sleeved *kimono* with a bright-colored pattern on the sleeves and skirt. But according to age and other circumstances the ordinary length sleeve is also used. The most formal attire of the bride is the *uchikake,* a white silk overdress, embroidered or of woven pattern, worn over the *furisode.* Sometimes during the wedding banquet there is a change of dress from the black wedding dress to an ela-

borately colored and designed *kimono* called *ironaoshi*
(changing of color), but this depends on the bride's
financial means and taste. The custom of changing
dress is one aspect of Japanese feudalistic vanity;
once upon a time there were brides who changed
three times during the banquet, and there was even
one bride who had twelve different *ironaoshi*, one
to represent each month of the year—and fainted
while changing into the tenth.

Nowadays, when a wedding ceremony is held at
a church, most brides wear foreign-style wedding
dresses; yet after the ceremony some of them
change according to the old custom from foreign
dress to the *furisode*, also donning a wig in the
Japanese hair style.

Formal Dress of Men and Women

The man's formal Japanese dress is a crested *ki-mono*, a *hakama* (divided skirt), and a crested *haori*
(Japanese-style coat). This formal attire is worn
for both wedding and mourning ceremonies.

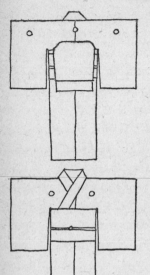

For felicitous ceremonies the woman puts on a crested *kimono* with a pattern on the skirt which suggests joyfulness. When attending funerals, women wear black with a crest but without a pattern. The *obi* (Japanese sash) is white with a gold or luxurious pattern for weddings and black without a pattern for funerals. In some areas of the country the people wear white *kimono* and white *obi* when attending a funeral. Young women, married and unmarried, may wear to a funeral a quiet-colored *kimono* with crest and without pattern together with a black *obi*. The quiet-colored *kimono* without a pattern is also worn when attending mass for the deceased. When the ceremonial *kimono* is worn, the *han-eri* (neck-bank) must always be white; thus the phrase *shiro-eri mon-tsuki* (white collar and crest)

has much the same meaning for us as "black tie" has in the West.

Dress for the Shichi-Go-San Festival

On November 15th boys of three and five and girls of three and seven years of age, dressed all in new clothes, visit a shrine to express gratitude for their health and to ask for future protection and happiness. This festival is called *Shichi-Go-San* (seven, five, three). The *haori* and *hakama* are the formal attire for boys, and the *kimono* with a design on the skirt for girls, but nowadays, in keeping with the times, foreign clothes are often seen in the cities. In fact the dress may be anything that is becoming to the little child.

Notes on Clothes in General

Mon-tsuki (crested garments) are classified in the following order of formality: five dyed crests, three dyed crests, three embroidered crests, and one embroidered crest.

Hadagi (underwear) must be worn even during the hottest season when one pays a visit or meets an elder. Wearing a bath-dress (*yukata*) without underwear is fashionable but not elegant; we should not visit in such costume. On calls, we must wear white *tabi* (socks); colored *tabi* are worn at home only. Of course we should not go out in a bath-dress tied with a narrow sash or in a *dotera* (padded dressing gown), although at hot spring resorts we do see people wearing these.

The *haori* was never worn before high personages in olden times, and in the present day also we do not wear it on formal occasions. There is a similarity here to the etiquette of removing one's coat at a house entrance. However, the black *haori* with crests is worn very often by aged women when expressing honor to others, visiting seniors, attending meetings, and also seeing friends off at the station or other such places. And, by the way, Japanese have a great reputation for seeing people off at stations.

Each Japanese family has its own crest which is handed down from generation to generation. When a woman marries, all the *kimono* which she takes with her to her husband's home bear the crest of her own family and are used indefinitely, but any *kimono* made after she is married bear the crest of her husband's family.

Among the different kinds of *kimono,* the *muji* (solid-colored) is formal, the *komon* (small pattern) informal, and the *shima* (stripe) very informal.

Kimono for the Young and the Aged

Bright-colored *kimono* with big designs are worn by young people, but older people dress more sedately. This is true also of the *obi* and accessories. The sleeves of an unmarried girl's *kimono* are long, but they become shorter as she grows older. Since the end of the war the *Genroku sode* or short sleeve has gained favor with both young and old; it is so called because this sleeve was likewise popular in the Genroku Era, roughly during the latter part

 of the seventeenth century. The shape in which one's *obi* is tied also varies according to one's age. *Tateyanoji* (vertical arrow shape) and the butterfly shape are for young girls while the *otaiko* (drum shape) is for adult women.

Chapter Seven

Marriage

From days of old, Japanese people have thought of birth, marriage, and death as the three most important and most sacred events in human life. Of these three it is marriage which is said to determine the course of one's life. Hence the following paragraphs concerning Japanese marriage customs concern one of the most serious aspects of our social life and should not be overlooked by anyone who is a part of Japanese society.

Parents earnestly hope for a suitable marriage for their children; in Japan, where the family system is still very strong, parents not only hope for this but take over all responsibilities in seeing that their children are prepared for life and happily married. This is especially so in the case of a daughter, as there is little occasion for girls to meet prospective husbands except under their parents' roof or in the homes of their friends. Relatives and friends of the parents, with deep consideration for the future of youth, come to the aid of parents at this time and do all that they can to help towards a suitable marriage. A particular function of a friend or relative is to serve as the *nakôdo* or " go-between," and though today as well as in the days of old there are many young people who find love themselves, marriages in Japan are generally brought about with the help of the *nakôdo* and only with the consent of both parents. Since the war, schools have become co-educational and more and more girls have begun to take positions; circumstances have changed greatly toward giving young people much more opportunity to meet each other. However, the old manner of arranging marriages still prevails in most families.

The Preliminaries

A *nakôdo* first makes sure in his own mind that the marriage which he proposes is likely to be a happy one, taking full account of the standing of the two families and the character and the age of the two young people. He than suggests the marriage to the two families. If the families are not acquainted with each other, they then study each other and the suggested bride or groom as to heritage, health, position, interests, and character. This is all done very discreetly and, finally, if everything appears satisfactory and the two young people are so disposed, the *nakôdo* arranges for them to meet personally by inviting the young people, with their parents, to a home or a play or a concert. This meeting is the important *omiai*.

A final decision is made after the *omiai,* based upon the feelings of the families and the young people. It is sometimes arranged that the two young people can associate with each other for a while and then decide the matter for themselves.

Once the difficult path of decision has been left behind, the way ahead is straight and clear. Yet along it still shine very clearly the white stones of etiquette to mark the path which one must tread. Since much of this concerns the ceremonial realm of etiquette, the most beautiful and glorious in one's life, we should like very much to go into detail, but the brief space here does not allow it and, as the details have to do only with the happy young persons directly concerned and can be observed when the occasion occurs, we shall limit this account to only those points most necessary for the observers to understand.

The *nakôdo* not only takes the responsibility for introducing the two families, but after the marriage is decided upon, assumes all responsibilities for the betrothal and wedding.

The Betrothal

When the marriage is decided upon, announcements are made to relatives, and a day is fixed for the exchange of betrothal presents, called *yuino*. Usually from the bridegroom-to-be comes a list of presents to be given, *obi* material or betrothal gift-money, a *suehiro* (a fan which broadens at the end, symbolizing more and more happiness), a list of the members of his own family, and a list of his relatives. From the bride-to-be will go similarly a list of presents, material for *hakama* or betrothal gift-money, a *suehiro,* a list of the members of her own family, and a list of her relatives. Of course in the present day other gifts are exchanged, perhaps even an engagement ring, but the traditional form of giving is always followed. It is interesting to note that nowadays the procedure in part is carried out only in a symbolic way. The gifts on the lists actually are not exchanged, only the *obi* and *hakama* material or, in their stead, the betrothal gift-money being actually exchanged. The lists, in fact, are part of the ready-made wedding paraphernalia outfits sold by department stores. With regard to the betrothal gift-money, it is customary for the bride's family to return to the bridegroom's family an amount equivalent to one-half of that received.

The betrothal gifts are taken on a stand made of bare wood, first from the bridegroom-to-be's home to the bride's home by the *nakôdo;* then the *nakôdo* takes the gifts prepared by the bride-to-be's home to the other home. In presenting the gifts the *nakôdo* greets the receiver with : *Ikuhisashiku medetaku gojuno kudasaimase.* " Please keep this with felicity forever." The receiver receives the gift saying : *Ikuhisashiku medetaku juno itashimasu.* " I shall keep this with felicity forever." And thus the betrothal pact is sealed between the two families. On the day of the betrothal the *nakôdo* is entertained at dinner at the homes of both families or made a present of cakes in joy of the occasion.

Such is the traditional way, but so greatly have circumstances changed by now that this part of the ceremony is often omitted or done in a simple way.

The Wedding

After the betrothal, the date for the wedding

ceremony is set by choosing a *kichi-jitsu* (calendar day of good luck), which, in most cases, is a day called *tai-an* (great peace).

The ordinary Japanese wedding is a Shinto ceremony, but there are also Buddhist weddings and Christian weddings. The Shinto wedding is held at a regular shrine or before a shrine set up in some ceremonial hall, being performed before Izanagi and Izanami, the god and goddess who gave birth to Amaterasu Omikami (the Sun Goddess), traditional ancestor of Japan. Before these two gods a Shinto prayer of promise to be faithful one to the other is made; then the sacred wine which has been offered to the gods is drunk from three wine cups by the man and woman in turn, three times each, and a pledge is made to live through life together. This is called the drinking of the *san-san-kudo* (three times three, nine sips) pledge. Often wedding rings are exchanged at this time.

Most Japanese weddings are attended only by the families and close relatives of the couple. If, however, a Westerner is invited, he need have no fear of being embarrassed inasmuch as there are always attendants on hand to guide and instruct those present.

After the wedding ceremony, there is a reception for relatives and friends. This, called the *gohiro,* may be a luncheon, tea, or dinner, according to the means and taste of the married couple. The reception is a valuable steppingstone to friendships and future social amenities for the newly married couple.

After the wedding, a gift of thanks within one's means is made to the *nakôdo* by the newly married couple, who always look upon their *nakôdo* as someone to whom they owe deep gratitude, and to whom they do not neglect their social duties.

Not very long after the wedding the newly married couple makes a round of calls upon those friends and relatives who wished them joy upon their marriage. After this, the new bride makes her first return to her own maiden home on a certain day. This old Japanese custom is called the *osatogaeri.*

On Receiving a Wedding Invitation

Unless it is a Christian ceremony, usually only close relatives are invited to a Japanese wedding, but friends are invited by the parents of both the bride and groom to the reception following the wedding. The invitation cards are white and bear the crests of both families. Ordinarily they are sent out by the parents of both families, but nowadays some couples send their invitations by themselves. When one receives such an invitation, one sends a letter of congratulation together with the return card accepting or regretting. Then, more than two days before the appointed day, a call is usually made to take a wedding gift. There have been traditional gifts, but at present we usually choose something that would be enjoyed in the new home, and when the bride or groom is a very intimate friend, we sometimes even give things for personal use. Sometimes separate gifts are given for both the bride and the groom. Actually the choice of a present is determined very much the same way as in the West. The way to wrap a wedding gift is explained in Chapter Four.

On the day of the wedding we arrive a little before the time set for the reception and are met at the entrance of the reception room by the bride and groom, the *nakôdo,* and the parents of the bride and groom, to all of whom we extend our congratulations.

Wedding receptions are usually held in ceremonial halls, reception halls in hotels or clubs, or often a home, usually, but not always, the groom's. After the formal reception we speak to the bride and groom again if they have not already left on their honeymoon, and bid them good luck; but we must never say *sayonara* because that means parting, and it is considered unlucky at weddings to use any word that suggests separation.

Chapter Eight

Deaths

Death with its sorrow and unhappiness brings us to etiquette which is more a matter of the heart than of rules. Death's sorrow is sacred, and man has surrounded it with certain solemn ceremonies, the exact nature of which depends upon the religious faith of the bereaved. Most families in Japan hold their ceremonies according to either Shinto or Buddhist rites, and one should bear in mind that there is a fundamental difference in the ceremony and spirit of Shinto, Buddhist, and Christian prayers.

In death again it is that portion of the room

immediately in front of the *tokonoma* which is considered the most honorable, and here the deceased is laid out, with the head toward the north but without a pillow. A white cloth is placed over the face, and the hands are clasped. A low table is placed at the head with the following offerings upon it : incense, flowers, and candles if in Buddhist style ; *semmai* (specially washed rice as an offering to the gods) and water if in Shinto style. A sword to ward off evil spirits is sometimes included. Simultaneously with this ceremony, a piece of paper inscribed with the characters *mo-chū* (in mourning) is pasted on the entrance gate, and if there is a god-shelf within the house, the doors of the shrine thereon are closed.

As in any other country, relatives and close friends are notified and, according to the religion of the bereaved, a Buddhist or Shinto priest or a Christian minister is called to make arrangements for the *otsuya* (wake), encoffining, and funeral.

The undertaker sets up an altar for the dead in the honor section of the home. The coffin and all articles necessary for the altar are brought by the undertaker, but sweets, vegetables, and other food offerings are furnished by the family. The favorite vegetables of the deceased are selected.

When all arrangements are made and the day of the funeral decided upon, notices are sent out to the friends of the bereaved. If the notices are not printed, letters are written to superiors and post cards to others.

Condolence Calls

Upon notification of a death, Japanese etiquette requires that one call promptly to express one's sympathy, permissibly even at night. Even without notification, one should call when one's professor or superior or close neighbor has died. When making such a call we take a gift for the deceased such as flowers, vegetables, or money, wrapped as indicated in Chapter Four.

The first thing to do upon calling is to pay respect in front of the coffin; afterwards express your sympathy to the family of the deceased. Of course, if you meet a member of the family on your way to the room where the coffin is placed, it is proper to express your sympathy then, but upon entering the room where the coffin is placed, always bow first before the coffin.

The way to pay respect to the deceased differs according to the religion of the deceased. Buddhist prayers are performed while offering incense. If the prayers are to be made while standing, one approaches the deceased to within three steps and prays, then moves to the incense-holder, where one clasps hands and bows, then burns incense in the holder —once, twice, or thrice. The incense, in powdered form, is grasped between the first finger and thumb, held up to the height of one's chin while performing a slight bow, and then placed in the censer to burn. Next, one retreats three steps and prays with the hands clasped, then again draws back about two yards to bow, and finally returns quietly to one's seat. To pay the same respects to the deceased from a sitting position, the procedure is much the same. One prays with the hands on the mat about three feet from the deceased. Advancing on the knees to the incense stand, one then burns the incense, retreats three steps, still kneeling, and prays respectfully. The rest is the same as for the standing ceremony.

In this Buddhist ceremony, incense sticks, as well as incense powder, are burnt before the dead, the sticks only being used when paying homage on a second visit. If a lighted candle is in use, the three sticks required are lit from it. If the sticks flare up, the flame is never put out with the breath, but by hand, after which each stick is lifted in honor, one at a time, before being placed in the censer.

In the Shinto ceremony, prayers are performed by offering the *tamagushi,* which is a branch from the *sakaki* tree. The branch, received from the priest, is held in both hands with the palms upward, the right hand grasping the stem and the left hand slightly supporting the leafy end. One advances with the leafy end pointing towards the altar and stops some few feet away from the shrine to pray and then approaches the *tamaguchi* table. Here one reverses the position of the branch so that the stem is pointing towards the altar and, in that position, places it upon the table. One then retreats, bows in homage, and claps the hands together twice—though the bow alone is sufficient. Retreating further, one pays reverence again, this time bowing more deeply. The formal custom is to clap the hands four times, but twice is sufficient when many other people are to follow. The worship over, one bows to the chief mourner and the priest before returning to one's seat.

Should there be a cushion in front of the coffin for the use of mourners it should be used even though it is not considered most respectful to the deceased to pay one's respects while kneeling on a cushion.

Since the Japanese way of paying homage to the deceased is complicated, it is sufficient for foreigners to express their respect in their own way — a simple bow before the altar would be quite sufficient.

Unless one is on special terms, one should not attempt to see in person any family members at this time. And those in mourning do not see people off. Also, one should never call on anyone else just after having visited a family where there has been a death. This is very much disapproved of in Japan.

Otsuya

After a death and before the funeral, vigil for the deceased is kept on one or more nights. This, called *otsuya,* is observed quietly by relatives and intimate friends of the departed only. If in Buddhist style, a priest is called to chant sutras. A light supper is served the guests around midnight. However, for others calling to express condolences, this occasion being exceptional, neither tea nor cakes need be offered, nor need callers be urged to stay.

Other Ceremonies

Ceremonies are held at the time of the encoffining, at the departure of the coffin from the home,
and during the cremation and burial. These ceremonies, together with the funeral described below,
are held under the direction of a Shinto priest,
Buddhist priest, or minister, so as not to overlook
any courtesies to the deceased.

At all ceremonies for the dead there is a distinct
order in paying homage to the deceased : first,
the chief mourner, then those members closest to
the deceased, then others in the order of their
arrival.

The Funeral

Funeral services are held at the ceremonial hall
of a great temple or cemetery, such as the one at
Aoyama in Tokyo, at a church, or sometimes in

the home. In the present day, funeral services are often attended only by near relatives and intimate friends, and others are asked to come only to the farewell ceremonies held at the end of the funeral services.

The Farewell Ceremony

At a farewell ceremony, you first check your hat and coat at the cloak room near the entrance of the hall, present your name card and incense fee, and then enter the ceremonial hall. After entering, you advance toward the coffin from the left. At a Shinto funeral you will accept the *tamagushi* from the priest at the coffin and use it as described above.

To the friends of the deceased, standing on the left-hand side, make a light bow when passing before them. When in front of the coffin, pray in the Shinto or Buddhist manner, whichever is the religion of the family, and then advance to the chief mourner and the family of the deceased and bow to

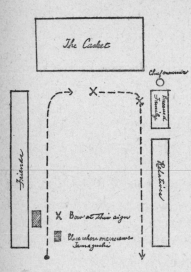

express your sympathy. The chief mourner will be standing nearest to the coffin on the right side, the family of the deceased in a line next to him, followed by the relatives of the deceased. After bowing to the chief mourner and the family, bow lightly as you pass in front of the relatives, and leave.

After the funeral, to all who attended the funeral and farewell ceremony, the family sends a letter of thanks on the very day of, or the day after, the ceremony. A personal call at the entrance is made to neighbors.

Chapter Nine

Flower Arrangement

Flower arrangement is an art that is an indispensable part of the daily life of the Japanese people. It is said to have originated from the custom of offering flowers to Buddha and the Shinto gods. However that may be, it certainly expresses the love that the Japanese people have for nature.

This art fits in most becomingly in the Japanese home, just as the arts of painting and sculpture suit the Western home. Simply by arranging a few flowers, we create an impression of natural life surrounding us and a sense of closeness to natural beauty, an integral part of the Japanese way of life.

The characteristics of Japanese flower arrangement are found in the beauty of the lines rather than in the harmonization of colors of the flowers as in the West. This is particularly so in the *seika,* a formal style of arrangement. The branch, the placement of the stalk, and the shape are considered before arranging the flowers to create a sense of beauty. This perhaps comes naturally from Japanese architecture, especially from the beautiful and simple lines of the *o-zashiki* (Japanese living room).

Styles of Arrangement

The styles of flower arrangement may be classified into three kinds : *seika,* a formal style ; *nageire,* an informal and natural style ; and *moribana,* the most modern form.

SEIKA STYLE — This is usually called *ryûgi-bana,* represented by the Koryu and Ikenobo schools, which follow definite forms of arrangement and therefore are considered to be formal, classical schools. The

length and angle of each
branch are strictly fixed
in the shape of an irregular
triangle called *ten-chi-jin*
(heaven, earth, man) which
gives a strong impression of uniformity and equilibrium.

MORIBANA STYLE — This style has no special form,
the flowers being arranged so as to create a natural
scene in miniature which harmonizes with the container. In the low, flat water-vases, baskets, and
wide-mouthed vessels used, the flowers are held in
place by metal spiked holders. This style is much
more modern and free than the *seika* style, for there
is no set form which must be followed.

NAGEIRE STYLE — This style, also, is not prescribed
by any rigid rules, and as the flowers are supported
by the rim of the vase, the arrangement conveys at
one glance the impression that the flowers have
been freely placed in the vase. However, it actually
conforms to rules and has dignity and harmony.

In the *moribana* and *nageire* styles, there are
different schools such as the Ohara, Adachi, Sogetsu,
and many others.

Flowers for Felicitous Occasions

Vases should be regularly shaped and pleasing to the eye. They may be of silver or bronze, or in the summer earthenware glazed in cool colors of green and white, sometimes set on stands.

Flower arrangements for New Year's and marriage ceremonies combine pine, bamboo, and flowering plum and are called *sho-chikubai.* However, when plum blossoms are not in season *omoto* (rhodea), *kiku* (chrysanthemum), or *ran* (orchid) may be used instead.

The following flowers symbolize joy : pine and rose, signifying eternal youth and long life; pine and *omoto* (rhodea), signifying eternal youth and eternity; pine and *botan* (tree peony), signifying eternal youth and prosperity; tree peony and bamboo, signifying prosperity and peace; *habotan* (cabbage flower); *fukujusô* (adonis); *senryô* (chloranthus); *manryô* (ardisia crenata); chrysanthemum; orchid.

During the Girls' Festival in March, flowering

peach, rape flower, and spring chrysanthemum are characteristic. For the Boys' Festival, iris is the special flower.

Flowers to be avoided on felicitous occasions are autumn flowers, maple, tea plant, flowers of purple hue, Japanese rose, *shakuyaku* (herbaceous peony), those that are inclined to wilt within a day, and those traditionally used on the Buddhist altar such as *shikimi,* a kind of evergreen. Moreover, in exchanging betrothal presents and during marriage ceremonies, not to be used are flowers bearing a name which includes the word " *saru* " meaning to depart, as in the flower *sarusuberi* (crepe-myrtle).

Flowers for Funerals and Memorial Services

Since on such occasions it is the custom to remove all elaborate decorations in the house, naturally no flower arrangement is used. However, just as for foreign funerals, white or light-colored flowers are offered, but never in the regular flower-arrangement way.

Etiquette Concerning Flower Arrangement

The correct position for a guest when viewing a flower arrangement is in a kneeling position about three feet away from the *tokonoma* (alcove). Bow politely and look at the arrangement, starting at the bottom and progressing gradually to the top, then quietly bow again and return to your former position. Looking from the side or peering into the vase is considered very rude.

If you wish to see the stem-ends of the arrangement, express the wish to your host, and then move closer to the *tokonoma*, the proper comment being : *Ikeguchi o haiken itashimasu.* " May I see the base of the arrangement?" This applies to occasions of visiting either a home or a public exhibit of this art. In the art of flower arrangement, a beautiful and orderly arrangement of the stems just at the base is most important and shows the skill of the arranger.

On going to view a flower arrangement in a

home, first exchange greetings with your host or hostess, then look at the flower arrangement on the *tokonoma* and compliment your host or hostess on the beauty of it, saying : *Omigoto na hana de gozaimasu koto. Haiken sasete itadakimasu.* "What beautiful flowers! May I have the pleasure of looking at the arrangement?" After viewing it, express your thanks and draw back.

When visiting a home on business, the business should be completed first before paying attention to the flowers.

You may look at flowers before the friend you are visiting enters the room, and then after exchanging greetings say simply : *Ohana o haiken sasete itadakimashita. Taihen omigoto de gozaimasu.* "I have had the pleasure of viewing your beautiful flower arrangement."

When the guest is moving forward to the *tokonoma* to view the flowers, the host or hostess sits near the post of the *tokonoma,* facing the guest. After the guest has expressed appreciation, with a bow, a modest reply is : *Ohazukashū gozaimasu.* "I am ashamed of my poor work." Then both the guest

~ 99 ~

and the host proceed back to their former seats. In general, flowers should be well-harmonized and balanced ; the lowest third of the arrangement must have stability. If the characteristics of the flowers themselves have been brought out vividly, it can be said that the arrangement has been skillfully done.

Chapter Ten

Tea Ceremony

"Teaism is a cult founded on the adoration of the beautiful among the sordid facts of everyday existence. It inculcates purity and harmony, the mystery of mutual charity, the romanticism of the social order. It is essentially a worship of the Imperfect, as it is a tender attempt to accomplish something possible in this impossible thing we know as life.

"Teaism becomes more than an idealization of the form of drinking; it is a religion of the art of life. The beverage grew to be an excuse for the worship of purity and refinement, a sacred function at which the host and guest joined to produce for that occasion the utmost beatitude of the mundane. The tea-room was an oasis in the dreary waste of existence where weary travellers could meet to drink from the common spring of art-appreciation. The ceremony was an improvised drama whose plot was woven about the tea, the flowers, and the paintings. Not a color to disturb the tone of the room, not a sound to mar the rhythm of things, not a gesture to obtrude on the harmony, not a word to break the unity of the surroundings, all movements to be performed simply and naturally — such were the aims of the tea ceremony."

Thus Mr. Kakuzo Okakura well explains the significance of *cha-no-yu,* or the tea ceremony, in his delightful book, *The Book of Tea.*

The formalities of the tea ceremony were instituted and brought to a high state of prefection by Sen-no-Rikyu, the greatest of all tea masters, in the sixteenth century under the patronage of Taiko Hideyoshi.

The Tea-Room

A tea ceremony is held in the *sukiya* (tea-house), which does not pretend to be other than a mere cottage — a straw hut. The first tea-room was created by Rikyu. The *sukiya* consists of the tea-room proper, designed to accommodate not more than five persons, the *mizuya* (anteroom), where tea utensils are washed and arranged before being brought in, the *machiai* (pavillion), in which the guests wait until they receive the summons to enter the tea-room, and the *roji* (garden path), which connects the *machiai* with the tea-room. It is smaller than the smallest of Japanese houses, while the materials used in construction are intended to give the suggestion of refined poverty. To the foreigner, because of the extreme simplicity and chasteness of its decoration, it may appear almost barren. But we must remember that the details have been worked out with care, perhaps even greater than that expended on the building of the

~ 103 ~

richest palaces and temples. A good tea-room is more costly than an ordinary mansion, for the selection of its materials, as well as its workmanship, requires immense care and precision.

Tea ceremonies were not necessarily always held in a *sukiya;* sometimes they were held in grand drawing rooms profusely decorated, but it was because Rikyu wished to warn people against extravagance and teach them the true spirit and worth of teaism, the love of simplicity, purism, and serenity, that he created the *sukiya.*

One thing very interesting about a tea-room is its small door not more than three feet high called *nijiri-guchi* (wriggling-in entrance). One must bend low and creep through it to enter the room; this procedure is incumbent on all guests — high and low alike — and is intended to inculcate humility.

Occasions for Tea Ceremonies

There are many different occasions on which a tea ceremony is held, but of course it can be held at any time when one wishes to have the pleasure of taking tea with those who share the love for this art. There are, however, certain set forms and occasions. The following are the seven forms :

SHOGO NO SAJI (Noon Tea) — This is the ordinary formal tea-ceremony party beginning with a *kaiseki* (a simple meal). The ceremony begins just at noon; one arrives at half-past eleven and stays till not later than four o'clock.

One should note that a tea-ceremony party almost always begins with a meal because of the nature of the tea used. This tea, called *matcha* (powdered tea), which has had the veins of the leaves carefully removed and is ground into a powder by the use of a stone mortar, is very strong and if taken without a preceding meal it would not be good for the stomach. This is particularly true when the tea is served with a thick consistency.

AKATSUKI NO CHANOYU (Sunrise Tea) — This is held around three or four o'clock in the morning. It is also called the *Zangetsu* (remaining moon) or *Zanto* (remaining lamplight) Ceremony, for it is held at a time when the moon still remains in the sky very early in the morning or when the lights in the stone lanterns still remain burning from the previous night. On this occasion, one never remains after six in the morning.

YOBANASHI NO CHANOYU (Evening Tea) — This is held when one wishes to spend the evening with company. It usually begins at six, and one may stay as long as one wishes because there will be no parties following. The word *yobanashi* itself means to spend the long evening together most leisurely.

ASA NO CHANOYU (Morning Tea) — This is usually held in very hot weather when it is more comfortable for the guests early in the morning while it is still cool. The guests assemble at six o'clock in the morning.

HANGO NO CHANOYU (After Dinner Tea) — This is sometimes called "Tea Ceremony and Cakes." No meal is served but only tea and cakes, and it can be held at any time of the day, usually about nine in the morning or one in the afternoon.

ATOMI NO CHANOYU — This is an occasion when one is invited to see the tea-room after some high personage or special visitor has been to take tea.

RINJI CHANOYU (Special Tea) — Referred to as the Moon, Snow, or Flower Ceremony, this party, in appreciation of nature, is held impromptu when nature is especially beautiful or a visitor has come from far away or a friend passing by drops in.

The above are the seven different forms of tea-ceremony parties, but besides these, ceremonies are held according to the seasons and special occasions. Those held according to the seasons are the *Kuchikiri no Saji,* which is a tea party held in the autumn when the pot in which the new tea picked in spring is opened for the first time, this being one of the most important occasions for a tea-ceremony party; the flower party; the moon party; midsummer, winter, spring, New Year's, New Year's Eve parties; and the *Yoba no Chanoyu,* which is a party held at the season of the year when the use of the kettle on the brazier is being changed to the hearth.

Tea parties on special occasions are those for celebrations, memorials, farewells, and the completion of a new tea-house.

There are many other kinds of tea ceremonies, such as a party in the rain or in connection with religious ceremonies, garden parties, or flower viewing. Sometimes students will conduct a gigantic tea party. Tea ceremonies differ, too, according to the guest, the purpose of the ceremony, the place, the method of cooking, and the kind of tea used. In fact, there are countless varieties of tea ceremonies, some of them more informal and without the meal described below. A person skilled in the art is one who is able to meet any of the varying situations with poise and ease. One may, of course, in conducting a tea ceremony, simply follow set examples, but since this in no way involves participation of the mind in carrying out the event, such mere copying is looked down upon. Practice makes perfect in this art as in any other, and it is only by holding many tea-ceremony parties and by attending many that one becomes a master.

Procedures

It should be noted that throughout the following paragraphs only the masculine word " host " is used and that the guest is always referred to as " he." This was done simply to avoid the frequent use of the awkward phrases " host or hostess " and " he or she." All of the information, however, applies to women as well as to men. But it is men, more often than women, who conduct formal tea ceremonies. A wife may assist with the serving at a tea ceremony conducted by her husband but does not otherwise participate. A husband, if present at a tea ceremony conducted by his wife, simply makes an occasional appearance but is not actually a member of the party.

A tea-ceremony party, in effect, amounts to spending the day pleasantly, partaking of a meal, and drinking tea together, with a group of perhaps five guests, seldom more.

INVITATION — The host sends invitations to his

friends. The guest, in turn, calls in person at his host's home two or three days before the party to express his thanks and acceptance. This is called *senrei* (expressing thanks beforehand).

YORITSUKI (waiting room for guests) — This may be either a little arbor in the garden or a little room of three *tatami* (straw mats), six by nine feet, in the host's home. Here the guests gather about fifteen or twenty minutes before the designated time and await the arrival of their host. In this waiting room the guests determine their positions, choosing the *shôkyaku* (guest of honor), who is either one who holds a high position in the social world or is the eldest of the group, the second guest, the third guest, and so on to the last, who is called *tsumekyaku,* one who is well acquainted with the art of the tea ceremony.

MUKAETSUKE — After the host sees that all arrangements in the kitchen, tea-room, and *mizuya* (utensil-room) are ready, he goes to the *yoritsuki* and greets his guests with one silent bow. This is called *mukaetsuke.* After the host has retired from the *yoritsuki,* the guests enter the tea-room in the order decided upon. Before entering, however, the guests must be sure to cleanse their hands in the basin of water prepared for this purpose.

NIJIRI-GUCHI — This is the opening into the tea-room, being only about two and one-quarter feet high. To enter, you almost have to crawl on your knees. Enter quietly, turning back to put your footwear in order so that it will not be in the next person's way. When you have entered the tea-room, go first to the *tokonoma,* bow, look at the *kakemono* (hanging scroll), bow again, and seat yourself where you will not be in the next person's way. After the last guest, *tsumekyaku,* has entered the tea-room, the guests are ready to take their proper places one by one, beginning with the *shôkyaku.* At this time the host comes in and exchanges greetings with each one of his guests.

SUMIDEMAE — This is the method of arranging the sticks of charcoal. The host arranges the charcoal in the burner, where he next burns incense. The guests then ask for the *kôgô* (incense case) for each to admire.

KAISEKI (preliminary courses) — First, the host

brings in separate dining trays containing the food and hands one to each guest. Each guest in turn advances a little and waits for his host to hand him his tray. Then, making a bow, he puts out both hands, receives the tray, moves back to his former place, puts down his tray, turns to the next guest and says: *Osaki-ni*. " Before you." After all the guests have received their trays, the host expresses his regrets that the food is imperfect, but hopes that they will try the food at leisure ; then leaves the room through a door leading to the *mizuya*. Next, each guest removes the covers of both the rice and the soup bowls, the rice bowl cover with the left hand and the soup bowl cover with the right hand. These covers may be placed to the left and right, respectively, of the tray or they may be fitted together, face to face, and placed at the right of the tray. The guest then takes up his chopsticks and is ready to partake of the soup.

Next, the host brings in a *chsôhi* (bottle of *saké*) and *sakazuki* (small cups used for drinking *saké*) and persuades the guests to drink. He last brings in a wooden rice container. Since this contains a bowlful for each of the five persons, the first guest takes off the cover, serves himself, and passes the container on down the line, the last guest putting it down by his side. Next, *wanmori* (clear soup containing fish with vegetables), *yakimono* (grilled fish or fowl), and *shiizakana* (cooked vegetables) are brought in. After having brought in these dishes, the host again begs the guests to take their time and says that he will be in the other room : *Dôzo goyukkuri, watakushi wa achira de goshôban itashimasu.* He then goes back to the *mizuya* to eat his own meal, which is the same as that of the guests.

About fifteen or twenty minutes later, after the host has finished the meal, he quietly comes back to the tea-room and clears away any empty dishes. He again appears with bowls of soup on an oblong tray. This soup, plainly flavored, called *hashi-arai* (to wash chopsticks), is served in very small bowls. The next dish brought in is a plate " eight inches square " of sea food and mountain food as relish for the *saké.* And again the host urges the guests to drink. Now the host and the guests chat with each other. After a little while, the guests ask for hot water, and using a painted wooden pot, *yuto,* the host prepares a drink by pouring hot water over toasted rice or rice cakes. The guests finally wipe their rice and soup bowls with their *kaishi* (the soft paper that guests at a tea-ceremony party always carry in the front folds of the *kimono*) and put them in their proper places. With this the meal has ended.

ADVICE AND SPECIAL POINTS — In the *kaiseki* form of dinner, since the food is served in small quantities and is very lightly flavored, eat everything that is served. Refraining from eating when urged to do so is very rude.

It may seem unnatural for the host to eat in a separate room, but this is simply a sign of respect for the guests. Such respect is also shown by the fact that the host has prepared the menu, cooked and served the food himself. A clever host will relate some entertaining incident or story every time he comes out to serve the guests, and thus make the time pass pleasantly.

CAKES — As soon as the trays and dishes have

been cleared away, cakes are brought in on individual wooden plates of *fuchidaka,* with special spikes like large-size toothpicks. The guest picks up the cake on his *kaishi* and eats therefrom. After finishing, the toothpick is wrapped in some paper to be taken home. The host then invites the guests to the *koshikake* to rest, whereupon they leave the room through the small doorway, one by one, in the order that they entered.

NAKADACHI — The *koshikake* is a small house built in the garden attached to the tea-room or the main house. Here the guests rest in foreign-style chairs and possibly smoke. Meanwhile, the host tidies the tea-room, changing the hanging scroll for a flower arrangement and getting the tea utensils ready for the ceremony. This is called *nakadachi.*

GONG AND NOCHIIRI — When the above preparations are completed, the host sounds a gong, and the guests again cleanse their hands and enter the tea-room as before. If there is no gong, the host comes in person to call the guests, making a silent bow just as in the *mukaetsuke.* This is called *nochi-iri* (to come in later).

THICK TEA — The guests first proceed to the *tokonoma* as before to look at the flowers, which in a tea-room consist of a very simple arrangement done in a single-stalk vase. Next, sitting at the side of the sunken hearth, the guests one by one admire the state of the fire and hot water, the *mizusashi* (water-vessel kettle), and the *chaire* (tea caddy), and then go back to their places. When admiring the utensils the guests must be careful not to touch them. Presently, the host brings in the tea-vessels, one by one, places each in the proper and convenient position for handling them in relation to his seat, and then sits down and prepares the tea according to the prescribed ritual, designed to reduce necessary motions to a minimum. *Koi-cha* or thick tea is prepared first. It is prepared in one big bowl for all the guests, and the bowl is passed around from guest to guest for each to drink in the conventional manner. This should create a feeling of intimacy.

HOW TO DRINK TEA — The first guest takes up a *fukusa,* a small piece of silk cloth about five inches square sewn double which was brought with the bowl. With the *fukusa* in his left palm he places the bowl upon it with his right hand. After nodding to the next guest with, *Osaki-ni,* "Before you," he turns the bowl once to the left, bringing the side without a design toward himself, and takes three and a half sips. Afterwards, he lays the *fukusa* on the *tatami,* wipes the edge of the bowl with his *kaishi,* and passes it on to the next guest Everyone drinks in the same manner. The last guest hands the bowl back to the host who, after washing it, again passes it to the first guest. Each guest admires the bowl. The first guest, on behalf of the others, asks the host about its origin and history. Likewise the guests inquire about the tea caddy, dipper, and bag. Looking at each article carefully and with interest is good etiquette.

THIN TEA — After thick tea has been taken and the tea-vessels have been looked at, there comes a course of thin tea. Before preparing this tea, the host puts new charcoal on the fire. For this course, cushions and tobacco trays are brought in to make the guests feel more at ease. Dry cakes are served with this tea. The guest takes the cake from the bowl with three fingers and places it on his *kaishi*. Thin tea is prepared for each guest one at a time but in separate bowls and may be sipped at this state in any way the guest wishes. When one is through, he wipes the edge where his lips touched, using his thumb and first finger, and returns the bowl to the host. The host washes the bowl with hot water and again prepares tea for the next guest, using a different bowl. After the last guest has had this cup of tea and the utensils have been put away, the tea-ceremony party has ended. In other words, when the host has withdrawn with the metal receptacle containing the water used to wash the bowls and the fresh-water vessel, and after the guests have expressed their thanks, they make their exits in order through the small opening. After returning to the *yoritsuke,* they prepare to go home.

KOREI — After three or four days the guests must

not fail to write a note of thanks to their host or, better still, call in person at their host's home to express their thanks. This is called *korei* (thanking afterwards).

This is only an outline of the procedure followed in a tea-ceremony party. It may seem confusing and precise, but it should not be so at all. The personal dress may be anything that is clean ; what to do is only to take things as they come. When you see something beautiful, say it is beautiful ; when doing something before someone else, excuse yourself with *Osaki-ni ;* and do everything in an orderly, reserved, and modest manner. This natural procedure followed in the art of tea ceremony is based on long experience through many centuries, there being a precedent for all of its aspects. Simple, modest, sincere feeling is an integral part of the art.

Chapter Eleven

Annual Events

Nothing expresses more fully the spirit of a people than the time-honored annual events that are observed in a country. In these changing times, the way in which each family observes Japan's annual functions differs somewhat from the past, and in some cases some of the old customs are not observed at all.

Some of the breaking away from traditional observances is due to their religious origin and the changing attitude now shown toward matters of religion. On the one hand children in Christian

homes do not like to be left out of the old non-Christian festivals, and on the other hand non-Christians are celebrating Christmas more and more in one way or another. In spite of all the varying situations we shall try to describe Japan's major annual events as they are generally observed today.

With regard to Japanese celebrations one basic modern change must be kept in mind : the change from the old lunar calendar, closely connected with seasonal climatic changes, to the solar calendar, which places events about one month earlier than the lunar calender. The lunar calendar, which was observed generally in Japan up to the Meiji Era, is still observed in many rural Japanese communities.

January

The very decorations typical of the new year

seem propitious. The *kado-matsu* (gate-pine, three bamboo trunks with pine branches) is put up in front of the house; a *shimenawa* (taboo rope, similar to a rosette) is stretched across the gate; and a *sambo* (little wooden stand) bearing a *kagami-mochi* (mirror of pounded rice cake — the name seems to have come from the round shape of ancient mirrors), with a lobster, seaweed, evergreen or fern, white-beam, dried sardines, and dried persimmons decorating it, is placed in the *tokonoma* of the chief room.

All of these decorations signify, for various reasons, good luck. A small decoration of straw is also hung in each room. These decorations are put up before the 30th of December and taken down on the 7th of January; thus, the first seven days of the year are called *matsu-no-uchi* (among the pines). It is generally during this period that people receive and pay New Year's calls; however, women's calls may be made throughout the month of January.

During the first three days, called *san-ga-nichi,* each household partakes of *toso* (sweet *saké*) and *zôni* (a kind of soup with pounded-rice dumplings and vegetables), and prays for safety and sound health throughout the year. During this period, *toso* and the special New Year's delicacies arranged in a *jubako* (a fitted tier of lacquered boxes) are served to the guests making a round of New Year's calls. A card tray is set out for guests who make calls only at the house entrance.

Following is an example of a New Year's greeting card message : *Akemashite omedetô gozaimasu. Kyûnen-jû wa iroiro osewasama ni narimashita. Dôzo honnen mo yoroshiku onegai moshi-agemasu.* " Thank you for your many kindnesses during the past year. I hope I may have your further assistance this year." The usual verbal greeting at New Year's, during the first three days, is, *Akemashite omedetô gozaimasu,* and any time

明けまして
おめでとう
ございます

一月一日
東京都目黒区下目黒
三ノ五八二
西脇都子

up until the seventh or tenth of the month one may use, *Omedeiô gozaimasu.*

The round of calls is generally made to superiors and relatives; to other persons only an exchange of New Year's cards is necessary. A present called *otoshidama* may also be given at this time.

January 2 marks the beginning of the everyday routine of ordinary life, when everyone does his *kakizome* (first writing, calligraphy), *hikizome* (first playing of music), *nuizome* (first sewing), and so forth. The first sweeping is also done on the second day. This is done because it is believed that if sweeping is done on the first day, the good spirits or omens which have entered the house will be swept out.

Tradespeople on this day decorate their horses or trucks gaily, taking them out for the first work of the year. This is called *hatsu-ni* (first load).

The first dream of the year is called *hatsu-yume,* and on this night many people sleep with pictures of treasure boats under their pillows—a custom similar in origin, perhaps, to the Western practice of sleeping on wedding cake.

NANAKUSA — On the morning of the 7th every-one eats a rice gruel, cooked with seven different kinds of chopped vegetables, to ward off evil spirits during the new year. Any vegetables on hand may be used now, but in olden days these were the *nanakusa* (seven herbs) — *seri* (parsley), *nazuna* (shepherd's purse), *gogyo* (Chinese-rape), *hakobe* (chick-weed), *hotoke-no-za* (Buddha's throne), *suzuna* (cud-weed), and *suzushiro* (white radish). In olden days the *nanakusa* custom was observed with great ceremony by every family, the master himself solemnly cutting the seven herbs on a chopping board. Nowadays this old ritual is seldom ob-served with so much ceremony.

KAGAMIBIRAKI: January 11 — The *kagami-mochi* or mirror-shaped rice-cake which was decorating the alcove during the New Year's celebration is cut and eaten in *zoni* on this morning.

AZUKI-GAYU (small-bean gruel) : January 15 — On this morning sweet gruel cooked with small beans is eaten to drive away evil spirits.

UTAGYOKAI HAJIME (The Emperor's Poetry Party) : January 18 — Since the tenth century there has been an annual party at which New Year's poems are read in the presence of the Emperor. Each year the Emperor assigns a subject for the poems. At first this party was only a court ritual, but since ten years after the Meiji Restoration ordinary citizens also have been permitted to submit poems, and a board of judges selects those to be read on this day. The poems are all written in the classic thirty-one-syllable form called *waka*. The poems of the royal family are read first at this party and then those of about fifteen commoners, who are invited to be present at this occasion.

February

HATSU-UME (First day of the February horse according to the signs of the zodiac) — On the first day of the Horse in February, a festival is held at the shrine of the God of Harvests, now not as frequently in city areas as in the country. This day, dedicated to prayers for abundant harvests during the coming year, was probably chosen because the horse on the farm is a most important animal and this is the time of the year when agricultural work is about to begin.

SETSUBUN — The day varies from year to year, but generally falls on the 3rd or 4th of February. By *setsubun* is meant the change of seasons, in this case the end of winter and the beginning of spring. On this night every house, temple, and shrine holds a ceremony called *tsuina* to drive out evil spirits with *mame-maki,* or bean-throwing. The beans are thrown to pierce the devil's eyes, so it is said in Japan. If it happens to be a year of the Ox, a man born in that year throws the beans while crying out : *Fuku wa uchi; oni wa soto.* "Good luck, enter ; devil, depart."

When the words "Good luck, enter" are uttered, the beans are thrown from the entrance-way into the house or building, and when one says, "Devil, depart," they are thrown out from the entrance. The same procedure is followed at the entrance to every room in a home. It is said that if one picks up and eats these beans, equal in number to one's own age, good luck will follow. It is an extra popular treat when a big *sumo* man (Japanese wrestler) throws the beans.

March

DOLL FESTIVAL : March 3 — During the latter part of February, a stand of five tiers is set up in the *tokonoma* (alcove). A red cover is spread completely over this stand, and on each one of the tiers beginning at the top are placed miniature figures representing the Emperor and Empress, the palace orange tree on the right, the palace cherry tree on the left, court ladies, five musicians, Ministers of the Left and Right, and servants. On

the lower tiers are placed screens, paper-framed hand lamps, dinner trays, chests of drawers, rectangular chests, and mirrors, all such household accessories being made in miniature, according to

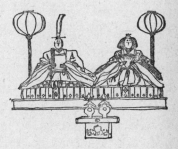

scale. White *saké, hishimochi* (diamond-shaped rice cakes), and varicolored parched beans are offered to the dolls, and dainty, pink peach blossoms are arranged near the stand. These preparations are made for the third day of the third month, a very happy occasion for a girl. According to an old saying, on the stand " put out everything that has eyes," that is, all the old dolls, even those that do not appear every day.

HIGAN — Higan, the Equinox, occurs twice a year, lasting seven days in spring and seven days in autumn. In the spring the equinoctial week starts at about the 18th or 19th of March and extends to the 24th or 25th. Since this is one of the annual events originating in Buddhism, every temple holds a ceremony during this week. The general public pays visits to the temples to honor their ancestors. The mid-day of the week, when day and night are of equal length, is called *higan-no-chūnichi.*

This equinoctial fete-day, also called *Shumbun-no-Hi,* is also observed in the Imperial Palace. The people in general observe the day by offering at the family altar such delicacies as *ohagi* (sweetened rice cake) and *gomoku-zushi* (rice mixed with vinegar and chopped vegetables).

April

KAMBUTSUE: April 8 — This is the birthday of the Buddha, who is known in Japan as *Oshaka-sama*. In the temples on this day a little shrine, with a small statue of Gautama placed in the middle of it, is decorated with flowers. Thus, this small shrine is called *hana-mido* (flower shrine). Worshippers pour sweet tea over the head of Gautama, and on their way back take some of the temple-brewed tea home with them to drink.

May

TANGO (Boys' Festival): May 5 — Just as the girls have their doll festival, the boys have theirs. Cloth carp and streamers are raised on poles outside

the house, and warrior dolls in helmets and armor are placed inside on stands. The flower used during this festival is the *shôbu* (sweet-flag), which is not only arranged on the stand but also thrust under the eaves of the house. *Kashiwa-mochi* (rice cake and bean jam wrapped in an oak leaf) and *chimaki* (cakes made of boiled rice) are offered to the dolls. It is on this day that the people bathe in *shôbu-yu* (a bath in which sweet-flag leaves are floated), to drive away evil spirits. Since the sweet-flag, with its upstanding, sword-like, and manly leaves, is the flower of the month, it is natural that it is used during this festival, but probably a more important reason is that the word for martial spirit, which boys are supposed to acquire, is also *shôbu*.

July

TANABATA : July 7 — This festival was first held to worship the Goddess of Weaving, but later came to be observed as a farm festival as well, the two being combined into a festival for weaving and farming. Then after a time the Chinese legend of two lovers, the stars *Shokujo* (Vega) and *Kengyû* (Aquila), was brought into this country and became connected with this festival. Little strips of colored paper with poems written on them are tied to bamboo sticks and hung out on doorways and under the eaves. The following morning they are taken down and set adrift on a river or the sea. This custom cannot be seen much in the cities now, but in the country it is still observed widely.

URABON (Feast of Lanterns): July 16 to 18 — This originated in the worshipping of the spirits of our ancestors. On the night of the 13th every faithful household lights a welcome fire for the spirits of the family ancestors, entertains them during the two days, the 14th and 15th, and on the 16th again lights a fire to escort them back to their graves. During these days, fresh vegetables and fruits are offered at the family Buddhist altar and lanterns are hung. All of these things, together with the send-off fire, are placed in miniature boats and launched on a river or the sea on the last day. During this whole *Bon* season the *Bon-odori,* a folkdance particularly associated with this festival, is a big feature, and, especially for the young people of the rural districts, is one of the happiest events of the year.

CHUGEN (Mid-year Day): July 15 — The 15th day of July, which falls during the Feast of Lanterns, *Obon,* is called Mid-year Day, *Chûgen,* after the Chinese custom. Presents are exchanged between relatives and persons to whom one is obligated.

DOYO: in July-August — *Doyô* is the Japanese name for " dog-days," the hottest period during summer. It is customary to eat eel on the Day of the Ox during this period as a prevention against summer ailments.

September

TSUKIMI (Moon-Viewing): on or around September 10 — According to the lunar calendar, the mid-autumn full moon rises on the evening of the fifteenth day of August, which falls on or about the tenth of September according to the solar calendar. At this time  an offering of new potatoes, dumplings, and autumn grasses is set up picturesquely on a stand in the moonlight.

HIGAN — As in spring, it is customary to observe the equinoctial week in autumn.

October

TSUKIMI : on or around the evening of October 13 — Moon-viewing is held on the evening of the thirteenth day of September (lunar calendar), complementary to the one held on the evening of the fifteenth day of August (lunar calendar). This time an offering of persimmons, chestnuts, dumplings, and soya beans is made. If one participates in moon-viewing on the earlier occasion and fails to do so at this time, it is said to be " one-sided moon-viewing, " and is not approved of.

November

SHICHI-GO-SAN (Seven-Five-Three): November 15 — Boys of three and five and girls of three and seven years of age, dressed in their Sunday best, are taken to worship at their patron-deity shrine. Prayers of gratitude are offered for their growth up to this time and prayers are made for their continued growth in the years to come. This custom was known in olden times as "the doing of the *hakama*" (*hakama-gi*) or "the untying of the sash" (*obi-toki*). On the way home one buys a long, narrow bag, highly decorated, containing *chitose-ame* (thousand-year candy) in long sticks to distribute among friends and relatives.

December

SEIBO (Year-End Gift) — As at mid-year *chûgen*, one exchanges gifts during this month with relatives and acquaintances.

TOJI (Arrival of Winter): about December 22 or 23 — The longest day in summer signified the arrival of summer, *geshi*. Likewise the shortest day heralds the arrival of winter. It is said that one can avoid catching cold during the entire winter season by eating pumpkin and taking a citron bath on this day. It need hardly be mentioned that the days become longer from this time on, but it is interesting to note the Japanese expression for this : *Tatami no me ga hitotsu zutsu nagaku naru.* " One by one each straw increases the length of the *tatami*."

NENMATSU (Year-end) — As has been described under January, one makes complete preparations for the new year by decorating one's doorways with straw festoons and making *mochi* (rice-cake) and other festive foods, which makes this the busiest time of the year for everybody.

OMISOKA (New Year's Eve) — At the shrines are performed what is known as the Great Purification, *Ôharai*, a freeing from all sins committed during the past year. The homes, too, undergo a thorough house-cleaning, *ôsôji*, both inside and out. This is also the deadline for the liquidation of all debts or loans.

At midnight one hears the ringing of temple bells, *joya no kane.* Each temple rings its bell 108 times. When they have ceased ringing we know that the new year has arrived.

Birth Festivals

Many ceremonial observances are held in conjunction with the birth of a child, but the following are the most common :

O-SHICHI-YA (Seventh Night) — The seventh day after birth is known as Seventh Night, *O-Shichi-Ya*. The child is named on this day, and in making the announcement a feast is given for those who have helped in connection with the birth. "Red rice," *o-sekihan*, is also distributed. It is customary, too, on this day for the bride's parents to send " birth clothes."

O-MIYA MAIRI (Shrine Worship) — The newborn baby is taken to the patron-deity shrine to have prayers offered for its growth, progress, and safety, thirty-two days after birth of a son, thirty-three days after birth of a daughter. Sometimes it is the midwife or wet-nurse or some other suitable matron who is asked to take the infant, dressed in holiday attire. On the way home from the shrine, one goes to the homes of friends and relatives to pay respects, and it is customary for the latter to celebrate the felicitous occasion by presenting small drums, *den-den taiko,* and toy dogs made of papier-mâché, *inu-hariko.* The parents celebrate by holding a feast.

TABE-ZOME (First Meal) — The hundredth or the hundred and twentieth day after birth provides another occasion for felicitation. The infant first partakes of rice on this day. A miniature dinner is prepared and fed to the child with ceremony, although actually only a single grain of rice is placed in the child's mouth.

TANJO (Birthday Anniversary) — Birthdays are celebrated very much as in the West. Relatives and friends are often invited to a dinner party, at which *o-sekihan* (red rice, so called because the rice is boiled with red beans) is served. The Western custom of giving birthday gifts is now frequently practiced. A child's first birthday is a particularly important celebration.

HATSU ZEKKU (First Annual Festival) — After the birth of a child, the first Doll Festival, *Hina*

Matsuri, in the case of girls, and the first May Festival, *Tango no Hı,* literally "fifth day of May," in the case of boys, is called the child's *Hatsu Zekku* and is celebrated with much festivity. At that time the infant is always given a festival doll or dolls to be used in making decorations for future festivals. Friends invited to the feast are given rice-cakes and *o-sekihan.*

Celebrating Longevity

KANREKI (Sixty-first Year) — Anyone who has arrived at his or her sixty-first year is said to have completed the sexagenary cycle and now returns to second childhood. He dons red leggings, similar to the old-fashioned soldiers' puttees which are wrapped around the legs, and a red Japanese coat, *haori,* and invites friends and relatives to a feast. When sending presents to such a person one makes it a point to choose something red. All of this is based on a combination of an old usage of the zodiac and the Chinese art of divination.

There are two sets of zodiac signs, one set having ten units and the other twelve. The ten units, which are referred to as "trunks," include the following : wood, fire, earth, metal, and water, each of which has its senior and junior unit, making ten in all. The twelve units, referred to as "branches," are named after the following animals : rat, bull, tiger, hare, dragon, serpent, horse, sheep, monkey, cock, dog, and wild boar.

The name for each year is made up with a trunk word and a branch word. Thus the first year in a cycle would be "wood (senior), rat," the second would be "wood (junior), bull," and the third, "fire (senior), tiger." The eleventh year would be "wood (senior), dog," and the thirteenth would be "fire (senior), rat." Progressing in this manner, the years would revolve around again to the identical name at the end of a sixty-year cycle, inasmuch as sixty is the lowest common multiple of ten and twelve, the number of units in the two sets of zodiac signs.

KOKI (Seventieth Birthday) — A familiar old saying is that "man lives but three score and ten."

Upon arriving at seventy years of age, then, in Japan one again invites friends and relatives to celebrate the important occasion.

KINOJI (The Festival of the Character " *Ki* ") — The seventy-seventh birthday is so named because the character *ki,* meaning happiness, appears to combine the Japanese characters with which the figure seventy-seven is written. Again one holds a festive banquet and distributes fans and silk gauze upon which the character has been inscribed.

EIGHTIETH BIRTHDAY — This is celebrated in fashion similar to the seventieth.

EIGHTY-EIGHTH BIRTHDAY — This is known in Japanese as the " rice " birthday since the character for rice appears to combine the three characters used in writing eighty-eight. Here again one holds a feast and distributes mementos.

National Holidays

At present we have the following nine national holidays :

SHINNEN (New Year): January 1 — On this day in the Imperial Palace the Emperor prays for the welfare of his country and people, and the people call to pay respect to the Imperial Family. Before the war in every home a similar service took place in front of the family altar. There is a three-day holiday to celebrate the new year.

SEIJIN NO HI (Coming-of-Age Day): January 15 — This day is celebrated in honor of those who have come of age.

SHUMBUN NO HI (Spring Equinox): around March 20 — Before the war this day was called *Shunki-Korei-Sai* (Spring Imperial Spirit Festival) and the Imperial Court paid respect to the spirits of Imperial ancestors. A similar ceremony called *Higan* was held at various Buddhist temples throughout the country. This custom is observed by many even now.

TENNÔ TANJÔ NO HI (The Emperor's Birthday): April 29 — We used to call this day *Tenchosetsu*, a word specially coined for the Emperor, but the government more recently decided on the more common words. *Tennô Tanjô no Hi* is literally

" Emperor's Birthday." People call to pay respects at the Imperial Household.

KEMPÔ KINEN NO HI (Constitution Commemoration Day): May 3.

KODOMO NO HI (Children's Day): May 5 — Before the war this was Boys' Day only. Now it is recognized as a day for all children, girls as well as boys. Welfare measures for children are given special consideration on this day.

SHÛBUN NO HI (Autumnal Equinox): around September 20 — As with the Spring Equinox, this used to be called the Autumnal Imperial Spirit Festival, at which time ancestors were paid homage at the Imperial Palace and in the local temples.

BUNKA NO HI (Culture Day): November 3 — This day was originally celebrated in memory of the Emperor Meiji, but now is called *Bunka no Hi* (Culture Day). On this day the nation honors those who have contributed to the world of literature, science, art, and sports, and the government announces cultural awards.

KINRÔ KANSHA NO HI (Thanksgiving Day): November 23 — This is a day of thanksgiving for the harvest, for the farmer who must work so hard, and for the working people. People who have worked for many years at one office or firm are honored at this time.

On these national holidays, public offices, institutions, and schools are closed, and the national flag is put up at the doors of houses and buildings.

These national holidays were established by the government after the war. Before the war we had other national holidays which also might be of interest.

Pre-War National Holidays

SHI HÔ HAI (Worshipping the Four Directions): January 1 — This was one of the four great holidays of the year. On this day the Emperor went out into the South Garden of the Shinkaden of the Imperial Palace and worshipped the Ise Shrine, the tomb of the Emperor Jimmu, the tomb of the preceding Emperor, and the great shrines and tombs in all directions, praying for peace and prosperity for the country. This ceremony is still held by the Emperor in the Imperial Palace, but *Shi Hô Hai* is no longer a national holiday.

GENSHI SAI (New Year Festival): January 3 — On this day the Emperor worships the Gods of Heaven and Earth and honors the spirits of the former Emperors. As in the foregoing case, the day is no longer a national holiday.

SHINNEN ENKAI (New Year's Banquet): January 5 — On this day the Imperial Court held a banquet for the Princes of the Blood, the Cabinet Officers, members of the Imperial Household, members of the Diet, other officials of rank, and representatives of foreign powers. All public offices, institutions, and offices were closed.

KIGENSETSU (National Foundation Day): February 11 — *Kigensetsu* was celebrated in commemoration of Emperor Jimmu, the founder of the Japanese Empire, who is said to have ascended the throne on this day 660 years before the Christian Era. The Japanese calendar began with this date.

CHIKYÛSETSU (Birthday of the Empress): The birthday of the present Empress was celebrated on

March 6. All girls' high schools throughout the country were closed.

TENCHÔSETSU (Birthday of the Reigning Emperor): April 29 — Still observed as a national holiday.

MEIJISETSU (Birthday of the Emperor Meiji): November 3.

SHUNKI KÔREI SAI (Spring Imperial Spirit Festival): usually around March 20, Spring Equinox — On this day the Imperial Court paid respect to the spirits of the Imperial ancestors. A similar ceremony called *Higan* was held at various temples throughout the country.

JIMMU TENNÔ SAI (Anniversary of the Death of the Emperor Jimmu): April 3.

SHÛKI KOR̂EI SAI (Autumnal Imperial Spirit Festival): around September 20, Autumnal Equinox.

KANNAME SAI (Harvest Festival): October 17 — This national festival honored the new grain which the Emperor offered at the Shrine of Ise to the Sun Goddess and the other Imperial ancestors. Special services were held before the Imperial Sanctuary.

NIINAME SAI (Second Harvest Festival): November 23 — The Emperor offered the first fruits of the new harvest to the Imperial ancestors, and also partook of them himself and shared them with the members of the Imperial Family and Household. The first *Niiname Sai* upon an Emperor's accession to the throne was called the *Daijôe* and was considered to be one of the most important festivals of the Imperial Court. Interestingly, this typical Japanese festival coincides, some years, with the American Thanksgiving Day.

Publisher's Postscript

We are well aware that in this book it is the standard etiquette that is described and not necessarily the everyday conduct of every Japanese. The Japanese themselves realize that in everyday practice, in Japan as elsewhere, there are innumerable instances when good manners are not displayed. They are chagrined over the matter and are doing what they can to minimize those instances.

On the other hand, all too often foreign visitors in Japan through their conduct have given many Japanese a false impression of what their home countries are like. It is true, of course, that what is shocking in one country might be considered commonplace in another. Lacking an understanding of such differences, and because of the language barrier, visitors to Japan have inadvertently and unintentionally, on occasion, shocked the sensibilities of many Japanese.

We ourselves fall into the category of visitors here and so feel we may be pardoned a few words concerning the conduct becoming ourselves and our Western compatriots—words which the dictates of good breeding and Japanese etiquette would never permit our hosts and authors to say. We do believe, however, that people who wish to understand the Japanese manner of doing things will appreciate having their attention called to such matters, and we emphasize that the World Fellowship Committee of the Tokyo Young Women's Christian Association is in no way responsible for our remarks. Coming right to the point briefly and bluntly, we are including below a few do's and don'ts which we believe the conscientious visitor should consider.

The Japanese are a friendly people and in many

ways they appreciate the friendly manners of Western visitors; however, there are some foreign ways that still seem strange and startling to them, for example backslapping and the taking of friends by the arm.

In conversation many Japanese are fascinated with American slang and figures of speech, but for the most part these are unintelligible to persons whose knowledge of English is limited to formal dictionary definitions. The use of pidgin English in no way facilitates a conversation and it invariably has a condescending connotation. Another thing to watch out for is the raising of one's voice when one is not understood. It is much better to repeat the statement two or three times slowly and distinctly, perhaps in different words, avoiding the appearance of barking.

Methods of conducting business in Japan are quite different from those in many other countries, and frequently exasperate the stranger. There is usually much irrelevant conversation and a great deal of negotiation; simple matters sometimes become very complicated and involved. Trying to rush things will in no way expedite matters. It is better to learn to sip tea and to appear as casual as possible.

Do not call a Japanese person "Mama-san" or "Papa-san." Few, if any, Japanese appreciate such appellations even when spoken with kindly intent. And under no conditions ever call an adult male "Boy-san." The Japanese respect age regardless of the clothing worn or the economic status of the person addressed. The term "Boy-san" is to be used only for bellhops and younger waiters. *Ano-ne* is a brief everyday word used in getting a person's attention and its usage is not considered impolite. *Gomen kudasai* is the simplest way of saying "Please excuse me" and is always a satisfactory way of introducing an inquiry addressed to a Japanese stranger. A waitress or servant may be addressed as "*nei-san,*" an old lady as "*oba-san,*" and an old man as "*oji-san.*" First names are used, if at all, only between intimate friends or for children, and in all cases the suffix *san* is added.

During Japanese meals Westerners sometimes commit errors which reveal their lack of knowledge of Japanese etiquette. For example, chopsticks should never be crossed when they are put down, nor should they ever be stuck into food and left standing there. *Shoyu,* which many Westerners relish, should not be poured over rice.

When visiting a Japanese home one should not show undue surprise at noting foreign-style household equipment and conveniences. To do so makes it appear that one considers the host or hostess " not as strange or barbaric as I thought at first." Flower arrangements and things such as art objects are of course to be admired, but to lavish extreme praise, giving the impression of saying, " Oh, if I only had that," places the host in a position where he feels he should offer the object as a present.

When entertaining a Japanese guest in your home, it is much safer to follow Western ways and etiquette for the most part. After all, it is the feeling of hospitality that really counts and your Japanese guest usually is more interested in seeing your way of life than a poor imitation of his own. A few added Japanese touches to make your guest feel at home will be appreciated, but they must be done correctly. For instance, a Japanese guest feels very ill at ease if he alone is served Japanese tea without the host and hostess also partaking themselves.

Do not express affection in public, even though your companion is a charming Japanese person. This simply is not done. Such displays invariably produce an unfavorable impression.

Getting fresh in public and annoying strangers is highly offensive. Being under the influence of liquor in no way excuses it. You can see many jovial Japanese after an evening's entertainment having a hilarious and sometimes noisy time as they proceed homeward, but for the most part their fun is restricted to their own little party.

One can get by in Japan with the wearing of almost any kind of clothing, but remember that loud and flashy styles are not approved of. At least in this respect the Japanese have not imitated their foreign guests. The wearing of such clothing places the wearer, in the eyes of most Japanese, in a class that in no way enhances his reputation.

At hot springs and public baths the modesty, or lack of it, which is shown differs considerably from that in some foreign countries. There are, however, some simple procedures to be followed, and it would be well to imitate those of any Japanese guests who happen to be present. In any case one does not cavort around as in a fraternity or athletic-club shower room.

Under appropriate situations moderate gifts of money are appreciated very much by servants, waitresses, bellhops, etc. Whenever possible this should be wrapped, even if only in a paper napkin or plain piece of paper. To offer money on the street to someone who has graciously helped one find his way is not proper. The desire to make foreigners feel at home and to help them find their way about is universal among the Japanese, and to offer a monetary reward for such kindness is a very poor way of showing appreciation. To pass out money on the street heedlessly and ostentatiously to the occasional beggar or urchin who happens by gives all the spectators an extremely false and un-complimentary idea of one's home country.

Whenever in doubt, remember the wisdom of the old saw, " When in Rome, do as the Romans do," or its Japanese equivalent: *Go ni haitte wa go ni shitagae.*